CW00551414

People who like dogs
like people who like dogs

People who like dogs like people who like dogs

Extraordinary encounters in an ordinary park

NICK DUERDEN

JOHN MURRAY

First published in Great Britain in 2024 by John Murray (Publishers)

1

Text design by Janette Revill
Illustrations © Alice Tait

A CIP catalogue record for this title is available from the British Library

Hardback ISBN 9781399818988
ebook ISBN 9781399819008

Typeset in King's Caslon by Palimpsest Book Production Limited,
Falkirk, Stirlingshire

Printed and bound in Great Britain by Clays Ltd, Elcograf S.p.A.

John Murray policy is to use papers that are natural,
renewable and recyclable products and made from wood grown
in sustainable forests. The logging and manufacturing processes are
expected to conform to the environmental regulations
of the country of origin.

Carmelite House
50 Victoria Embankment
London EC4Y ODZ

www.johnmurraypress.co.uk

John Murray Press, part of Hodder & Stoughton Limited
An Hachette UK company

For the afternoon crew

No man is an island

John Donne, poet, 1572–1631

Woof

Common canine expression

Author's Note

This book is based on both a true story and true stories. It's inspired by my experiences as a first-time dog owner, and conversations with the many people I encountered at the park, each of whom brought with them their own lives and narratives, which they seemed keen – on occasion, a little *too* keen – to share. Names, locations, events and some other details have been changed to protect the privacy of those mentioned, and in places I have incorporated events recounted to me by some of those I met. But their spirit, wisdom, and the friendship they offered is entirely real. I'm grateful to every one of them.

One

There is of course no empirical science behind the suggestion that dogs and their owners come to look like one another, but only a contrarian could deny that the resemblance between Sid and Rocky is a powerful one. As they walk effortfully towards me, I see a round man in his mid-fifties, with a round head and rounder stomach, and a heavyset bulldog whose own stomach doesn't stop where it rightly should but which rather has sunk all the way to the bottom of his legs, propped up there by two pairs of sturdy ankles. Both have faces that seem comprised largely of knuckles, their respective skin pulled taut over knobbly skulls, and suffer similarly from a raging eczema. Each gives off the impression that they

1

are fond of sausages; each boasts the most disarmingly becoming smile.

Sid, ostensibly the more human of the two, is confined today on his motorised scooter. Sometimes I see him here with a cane, at other times on wheels. Rheumatoid arthritis, he's told me, made complicated by obesity, diabetes and a pulmonary condition he did explain once, and which sounded complicated. It's quite the machine, his scooter, metallic blue, full of stickers, and it handles corners like a motorbike. Rocky waddles with earnest enthusiasm somewhere behind him. Despite a physiognomy that does restrictive and dreadful things to his own breathing ability, Rocky is the sporty type. He normally arrives in the park with a basketball which he dribbles across the grass with the kind of flair I'd more readily expect from those clever animals on TV talent shows. Sid has explained that he has never trained him, that this is simply the breed's natural inclination, to chase a large ball, and to keep it no more than a few millimetres from his snout. There is no transferable skill to this, and no real point, either. It simply is what it is: fun for him, excellent spectator fare for us. He follows his ball at an impressive clip for up to five minutes at a time, before reliably collapsing heavily onto the grass beneath him, abruptly exhausted, tongue unfurling from his mouth at length, like the red carpet at Cannes.

Today, the basketball is absent, and he is simply waddling to keep up, wheezing like a broken gas pipe, rivulets of saliva elastically suspended between jawline and the ground below. Sid sees me and lifts his meaty left hand up in a fleeting gesture while motoring ceaselessly forward. 'Can't stop, mate,' he says, 'not today, in a rush. Next time, yeah?' He turns awkwardly towards his dog. 'Rocky, come. Keep up.' I wave back, reminded once more that in this small neighbourhood park that's already reliably filled with unlikely sights and unexpectedly memorable characters, Sid and Rocky are practically tourist attractions. They could sell tickets.

It's mid-afternoon, another day much like the last, and the ones to come. The sky is overcast, a grey swirl of heavy cloud cover, the grass beneath my feet soft and patchily green, edged with the football paint for the matches that take place here at weekends. The Sunday leaguers don't like the dog walkers, and the feeling seems to be mutual. The latter aren't happy at how the studs ruin the grass, the former furious at all the dog shit that so many walkers here fail to pick up. Letters have been sent to the local council in common complaint. There is a section on the council's website especially for such grievances, encouraging both factions to simply get along. This appears an optimistic wish.

The grass isn't just shit-strewn, of course. Right now, in the middle of the week, it's also littered with takeaway remains left carelessly from the night before, and dozens of empty nitrous oxide canisters. But then the discarded chicken bones are the main reason why so many of the dogs agree to be walked here in the first place. They're like detectorists, foraging for the choicest discoveries, and oblivious to the dangers of those bones that get stuck deep inside gullets. The local vet does a brisk business.

It's a little after four o'clock, and I'm alone with Missy, walking the park's perimeter on what has, this past year, become an integral part of my daily constitutional, and which allows me to make up at least half the required steps I'm supposed to take each day but never quite do. It's mid-March, and cold. Missy walks by my side not because she is a particularly obedient dog, because she isn't, but because in my right hand I hold a treat, a twisted stick of something that smells vaguely like meat, which she likes very much, and for which she will follow me on endless laps in the hope of another bite. From a distance, this can be mistaken for loyalty.

Up ahead, I see several familiar faces and their reliable plus-ones, one of which is Tupac, the magnificent Akita the size and heft of a Shetland pony and whose presence alone makes at least two nearby Shih Tzus yap in admirable, if woefully ineffective, self-defence. The dog roams the far edges of the park on his impossibly long legs, and looks so exotic here I can't help but feel a more natural habitat would be an African savanna, rather than this suburban patch of green scrub. Tupac is a lone animal, though he belongs, at least notionally, to Benji. I've spoken only briefly to Benji in the past, always in passing, confusing conversations comprised of non-sequiturs and inexplicable flights of fancy, his not mine. When early on I asked him his dog's name, he responded that he didn't know because, 'he's never told me'. But in the many months since, I've heard him call out to the dog, putting excessive emphasis on the first syllable: 'Tooo'.

Benji might be in his early twenties or late thirties, it's difficult to tell. He favours a *Star Wars* T-shirt, and is obsessed with everything to do with Japan, this despite never having travelled further, so he's told me, than

Cherbourg (a school trip). When he does take notice of me, which doesn't always happen, he likes to say hello with an *arigato* and a bow from the waist. Today, he is drawing leisurely on a spliff while indulging, as he does most afternoons here, in what he has told me is called Bōjutsu, a martial art comprised of stick fighting using something called a *bō*, the Japanese word for staff.

'This isn't a proper *bō*,' he's pointed out on more than one occasion, 'it's just a piece of wood. But I love that name, don't you? *Bō*. I love that little flat line on top of the o, the accent. It's like it wants to squash it, but it can't because the o is too . . . too sure of itself, has too much composure, you know?'

I envy Benji his sense of wonder at the world around him and imagine him a practitioner of mindfulness. I once asked him what it was about Bōjutsu that appealed, when it always seemed a skill that lay ultimately beyond his ability. He looked confused by the question, shrugged, then pointed to Tupac, who was snuffling over by one of the more distant trees at the park's boundary. 'Do you have any idea how much he eats every day? Costs me a *fortune*.'

I watch him go through the motions of slashing and swinging and stabbing with his stick. He drops it frequently, but then it does look complicated, and Benji is clearly very stoned. His movements remind me of those fight scenes in the film version of the T-shirt he always wears, Darth Vader and his son, and those bright neon sabres. Despite his size and girth, because Benji is squat and a little overweight, he cuts an elegant figure, balletic and almost weightless on tippy toes, and he appears as oblivious to the cold – he wears no coat – as he does to

5

his dog, which I see now has broken out into a horsey canter, which makes his thick tortoiseshell coat ripple and shimmer. Head held high, Tupac cleaves a path through the gaggle of schoolchildren recently unleashed from the school gates across the road, and prompts intermittent screams from concerned mothers as they pull their young in close. Benji remains oblivious. '*Haar*,' he intones meditatively, eyes closed. '*Sheee.*'

He is out of his trance by the time I reach him. He opens his eyes and takes me in with unexpected interest. He removes the spliff from the side of his mouth, and for a moment I think he might offer it to me. Instead, he smiles disarmingly, and instantly I see what he must have looked like as a child. It makes me wonder about his mother. Where is she, in his adult life?

'Bruv,' he says, 'you couldn't lend me a tenner, could you? I see you here all the time, regular as clockwork, and you see me, so you know I'm good for it. Make it twenty, and I'll pay you back next week, no worries.'

The rain that had been threatening since I got here arrives now, as does the physical exhaustion that has been waiting to strike for the past hour. It always takes me by surprise, but shouldn't, not really, not now. It's an exhaustion that bears no comparison to the sort of tiredness I used to feel when my health was still mostly optimum, the kind everyone feels after a long day. This is different. It's more comprehensive, more total, and is brought on not by habitual exertion but rather the sad fact that my energy levels no longer renew as effectively as they once did and still should, and whose likely genesis lies in an old autoimmune issue that has left my body unreliable, and prone to setback. It will make the walk back home heavy, and long, and difficult, all the more so because I will work hard not to telegraph the sensations to any onlookers, nor to the dog, whom I do not want to disappoint. I will manage not to collapse into it until I get through the front door, and I know that the sensation will take many hours to lift, and that I will have to subject myself to early-evening television in a stupor before it does, the night passing like treacle.

But I know also, by now, to look on the positive side, that state of mind is important here, in terms of recovery, and sanity. And so I know that I will be here again tomorrow with Missy regardless, figurative small steps leading over time, I hope, to bigger ones, this daily constitutional now an intrinsic part of what more than one doctor has called my rehabilitation, 'both mentally,' she pointed out, 'and physically.' Nobody within the medical profession seems to know quite how to cure this condition of mine, which I'm told is mysterious and, depending on who I consult, is either nameless or else possessed of several contradictory names. Either way, improvement *is* possible. I have been told this repeatedly. The internet suggests otherwise, of course, and so I no longer consult the internet. If I'm going to maintain a certain level of self-belief here, then positivity is required. It is the dog that keeps me focused, and in part why we got her in the first place. It is for her that I click 'save' on my work every afternoon before heaving myself up out of my office chair in pursuit of gentle exercise, a gradual improvement in fitness levels, and more mental distraction than I might have bargained for.

Up ahead of me, Missy is writhing on her back, imprinting upon her fur a comely scent she has just this minute discovered, which I know I will have to wash off later with lukewarm water in case it proves to be something noxious. It would be rude to interrupt her, and so I don't. I wait until she is done, then call her, once, and watch with pride as she springs from her spine to her feet in an instant, and then casts a gaze around before spotting me, and comes sauntering over. En route, she falls into step with Tupac, of whom she is largely suspicious and so keeps at a respectably wary distance. Hard to believe they are the same species; he is four times her size. I say goodbye to Benji, and he thanks me, folding the note – a ten rather than the desired twenty: I'm not made of money – into his front jeans pocket, before falling to his knees to Eskimo-kiss his animal, who responds with a yoga pose, the only one he knows: downward dog. His tail shoots up, and causes the air around it to ripple, sending raindrops back up from where they came.

We make our way back towards the gate, the route so familiar to both of us after a year of this that we are by now on autopilot. I see Elizabeth and Pavlov in the distance, my daily walking friends, but I don't have the energy for them right now, and hope that Pavlov doesn't call me over.

He calls me over.

'Nick, my friend,' he says, and because this is early on in our relationship, I still notice his use of the word 'friend', and marvel privately that I am its recipient. These two, Pavlov and Elizabeth, people I'd never have encountered anywhere but here, are my familiars, supporting characters in the slowly developing story of my midlife. I swallow my torpor, find a brave face, and bid them hello.

'Look,' he says, 'like I am saying to Elizabeth, is nothing to worry about, yes?'

I am often struck by the fact that so much of Pavlov's daily narrative takes place in the complicated privacy of his inner thoughts as much as it does out loud, and that he sometimes gets confused about what he has spoken to me and what remains swirling around his head. I look to Elizabeth to help make sense of this conversation that clearly started before they saw me, and will likely continue long after I've gone, but Elizabeth, the beta to his alpha, is keeping dutifully quiet. She shrugs her shoulders, and we exchange a conspiratorial smile. For the next half hour or so, I am not focusing on how I feel but rather on this exterior concern. Therapists would say that from a recovery point of view, this is good for me.

'Olivia,' he says, as if this single dropped name explains it all.

'Olivia?'

'Yes, yes. Olivia. Earlier, we see her, and she is crying. But she shakes us away in that way she has, and walks off, you know? Has headphones on, says she doesn't want to be disturbed.' He explains that Elizabeth had wanted to go off in pursuit to make sure she was all right, but that he'd prevented it.

'Next minute,' he says, 'Olivia is calling us over, laughing and smiling now, and wants to tell us something funny she heard last night. She hugs Elizabeth, and she kisses me *here*.' He points to his cheek with the stub of his index finger, its nail bitten down to the quick, as if the clear skin somehow contains upon it proof of his claim. 'And I must say,' he adds, 'was very funny story, about some theatre producer she knows.'

'It was,' Elizabeth grins, nodding in agreement.

Olivia, a more peripheral supporting character here, is also one of the more memorable ones, a young actor with a necessary taste for the dramatic. Like Pavlov's, her inner thoughts thrum constantly with activity, and she does hot and cold with the most beguiling mystery. I think she's great.

Elizabeth doesn't like it when we dawdle for too long in one place. She's here to exercise, she reminds us, to keep her joints supple. 'A necessity at my age.' She cajoles us now into forward motion, and in this way I find myself helplessly swept along, Missy following faithfully in the slipstream of their own dogs, Dog and Betty, these ageing canine stalwarts who carry themselves with an air of quiet authority around here. Pavlov says that he saw something on the news last night which merely confirmed to him the fact that the world is beyond repair, and that billionaires are mostly to blame. He needs to tell us precisely why this is so, and he does – at length. The park is the place to vent, and Elizabeth's role is to listen, mine too.

I power on through my exhaustion on the lowest setting my battery currently has, and this is fine because Pavlov is older than me, and Elizabeth older than both of us. Nobody here is in a hurry. But when at last we complete another circuit and approach my gate (each of us has a separate gate from which we enter and exit), I make excuses firmly enough for Pavlov not to challenge me, and wave them goodbye.

'Tomorrow,' Pavlov says, in mock warning, 'we shall discuss AI, yes? I have some thoughts.'

I catch sight of Keith on his own dutiful circuit up ahead, dressed as ever in all white: white jeans, white shirt and jacket, daringly white cowboy boots. His Alsatian, which is albino, trots dutifully alongside him on its heavy lead, while the white cockatoo perches silently on Keith's left shoulder. There is so much I want to know about Keith, but the man remains a mystery. I wave to him, but if he sees me, he doesn't acknowledge the greeting, his eyes concealed as always behind a pair of vintage Ray-Bans, which are black and make for quite the colour contrast. I admire as ever his enviable posture, which is upright and erect, and admire, too, his fabulously swept-back hair. I am desperate to strike up a conversation with him, to learn his story in the way that so often seems permissible here between strangers when out walking their dogs, but this has never happened, not yet. He walks with such purpose and intent that I feel it would be rude to interrupt him. It was Pavlov who told me Keith's name, because Pavlov has a way of ingratiating himself with everyone, whether they'd like him to or not. But Keith keeps mostly to himself. I long ago decided that he's an old rock star, and I place him somewhere in his late sixties, ageing but handsomely preserved in the way that some rock stars are.

I leave the park just as the traffic lights are turning red, the cars lining up in front of them all clearly impatient to move, for the race to resume. The rain is pouring now, impossible to ignore, as is my woeful lack of preparation for it, the umbrella at home in the cupboard under the stairs. Droplets streak across the lenses of my glasses. I wrap the lead tightly around my fist, pull the dog in close, and then our combined six legs make a mad dash for it.

The following day, I've revived sufficiently that when Missy sits in front of my shoes, under the sofa where I'd carelessly discarded them yesterday, and paws at them with great unsubtlety, I put them on and locate the lead. The park is empty, the rain heavy enough now to have kept even the hardiest of regulars away but not, it seems, us. I need the exercise, the regularity of it, and, besides, what else would I be doing? I used to travel a lot for work, every month, so many airmiles to distant cities all too eager to reveal themselves. But my world has shrunk since then, and comprises just these couple of acres, give or take, within which my adventures are now restricted, quarantined between the trees and the bins, the gates and the benches, and beneath a sky that can never quite make up its mind whether or not to play nice.

Missy, still, at thirteen months old, comparatively new to both me and the world, is not put off by a little inclement weather. A Border terrier, she has a stiff wire coat that's better at deflecting the rain than any jacket, and boasts the energy of a just-lit firework; if she doesn't get to expend it, there are consequences. I watch her aquaplane with glee across the park's slippery surface,

in search of bountiful distraction. From out of the murk
and gloom, a cockapoo materialises, blond and, in a literal
sense, sheep*ish*. (He looks like a sheep.) Together, they
Torvill and Dean with such enthusiasm that it prompts
both owners into their orbit, making instantaneous
companions out of total strangers – as, so I'm learning,
dogs tend to do. Within fifteen minutes, this stranger, a
man, will cry openly in front of me. The park can be a
curiously intimate place at times, and learning its
etiquette is an ongoing process. Things that wouldn't be
permissible out there, beyond the gates, are fully accepted
in here, and so the strangest, most unlikely connections
are made.

While the rain seems to run off *my* dog, on *his* it sinks,
then swells into a million individual droplets, where they
sparkle like Christmas baubles. Each time the dog shakes
itself, it becomes a living art installation.

'Amazing,' I say to the man, and he beams back with
paternal pride.

Both of us have our hands thrust deep inside coat
pockets in the accepted male way. I pull the rim of my
baseball cap lower down in the hope of keeping rain
away from my glasses. His are liberally streaked.

'I need windscreen wipers,' he jokes. 'But, no, I've
always loved the rain. It's so refreshing.'

We fall into comfortable chitchat that the weather fails
to dampen. He tells me unprompted that he works in
online advertising, and that he found the sudden requirement to work from home an ideal situation due to his
being shy, a loner. I tell him that I've always worked
from home, and if I don't say much more yet it's because

13

some people make for better listeners. He tells me that his girlfriend was the more outgoing of the two, the extrovert. She was used to office life, and daily water-cooler moments that he was singularly failing to provide for her.

'Well, my *ex*-girlfriend, I should say. She left last week. We're taking some time, you know, some time apart.'

Each had worked from the kitchen table initially, but after a while she'd gravitated upstairs to the bedroom with the good laptop, and the router nearby. They would meet for lunch, walk the dog together, still a puppy, and then would return to the mounting pressures of WFH, and their inescapable proximity to one another.

'Netflix in the evening, but we could never agree on what to watch.'

'It happens,' I agree.

She'd taken to sleeping with her back to him, and was growing exasperated by his anxie*ties*, he said, emphasising the plural. The more he tried to rein them in, the more they multiplied, the tics and twitches, the itchy uncertainty he felt at all times that she hadn't closed the freezer door properly and that the food within – prawns! – was going off. He always had to go and double-check.

'I worry over everything, and the news headlines weren't helping, you know?'

They began to bicker, and then to argue, 'which is one up from bickering,' he laughed, telling a joke I felt he must have told before. I looked up at him and saw crows' feet, pain gathering at the corner of his eyes. 'She couldn't hack working from home any more, and so went back to the office despite everything.' Soon, they were taking the dog on walks separately, and the dog found himself almost always walking somewhere, with someone. 'We really tired him out, I think. But he loves it.'

At work, despite precautions, she got ill, came home and then, after a few days recuperating, packed her things and was collected by her parents. 'So that's it, pretty much. She's just *gone*. She called after a few days to tell me that she didn't think she was coming back. I don't think I saw it coming, not really. I thought we were just taking time out. I didn't realise it was permanent.'

Her plan had been to take the dog. It was *their* dog, though she had been the driving force behind its adoption, from Romania, and had paid for it too, via PayPal, to an organisation he couldn't help but worry was actually legit, and which she had insisted, more than once, *was*. They tracked its progress together, in the van, across the continent, via a pulsing dot on their shared iPad. It had taken seventy-two hours, including pitstops, and then the dog, Boomer, arrived, haggard and thin, watchful and wary, but with these big chocolate-drop eyes and a tail that had been cruelly hacked off at its base. Whenever Boomer wanted to show contentedness, his entire backend rotated counterclockwise.

'It was love at first sight. She's twenty-eight, my girlfriend, and I think she channelled all her maternal instincts on the dog. She doted on him. But I loved him too, you know?'

Boomer is the only thing they squabble over in the ongoing separation settlement. He tells me that she got most of the books, and that he was left with the vinyl. 'Do you like underground jazz of the 1960s?' he asks, not waiting for an answer, which is just as well. 'We went half on the furniture, but most of it is still with me because her parents, they don't have the space. Also, her father's allergic to the dog. We were together six years, were going to get married and everything. Kids, I mean. At least, I thought we were.'

I tell him I'm sorry.

'But I think she's seeing someone else now, a colleague. That's why she wanted to go back to work so soon.'

He looks down at his dog, at Boomer. 'I'm not giving him up, not now. I just can't.'

The rain pours steadily, and so I suggest we walk, as if by doing so we might just leave it behind. We walk on the stone path at the edge, at first stepping over and then helplessly into the expanding puddles, across the road from the swimming pool that closed last year for redevelopment and which won't reopen for at least another six. Behind us, the dogs follow at their own pace. Dotted around the park is the council-installed gym equipment, free for all to use: the bench press, the parallel bars, the rowing machine and the step master. Right now, half of them are ringed with industrial yellow gaffer tape upon which reads DO NOT CROSS. Some new graffiti has appeared on the football hut overnight, in praise of the ongoing efforts of doctors and nurses.

Dusk arrives early, hastened perhaps by the low clouds, which have turned the sky from dishrag grey to a brooding black. This brings with it the nightly avian rush hour, hundreds if not thousands of electric-green parakeets on the daily commute from the nearby royal park with its hills and valleys, its great oaks and its shimmering lakes, to a tatty patch of green just beyond *this* park that sits alongside a bus stop used in the afternoon by schoolchildren, and at night by drug dealers. I've never understood why they flock here. Why leave an area of outstanding natural beauty for something quite so palpably miserable? They make for a fascinating sight each afternoon, turning the skies dark, and making the most fantastic racket as they squawk the day's news to one another. I know nothing about birds, and nothing about nature in general really, having always lived in the city and revelled in it, but I love watching this sudden blanket of bright green and the accompanying noise. In the summertime, when we are required to sleep with the windows open, they wake us up at dawn on their commute *back* to the royal park, and then I don't like them quite so much. I lie in bed, vividly awake, imagining buying a shotgun and shooting the bastards, one by one.

'He misses her even more than me,' the man tells me, pointing to Boomer, who is trotting at his side now, all wet and fat. 'My girlfriend calls every evening to speak to the dog, and I have to hold my phone up to him while they, you know, *talk* on FaceTime. I don't think the dog can actually see her, but he does hear her voice, and I swear to you it breaks his heart. He howls, he actually *howls*. It hits me every time,' he says, thumping his chest. 'He hears her voice and he cries because he misses her, because he misses *us*, together, you know? And then of course that sets her off too, my girlfriend, who bursts into tears, and then I'm crying along with them.'

Looking across at me now, he laughs. 'So there we all are, all three of us, all heartbroken, in tears every night. It can't be healthy, right? And once she's hung up, Boomer sulks. He goes to his bed and curls up on himself. It's the saddest thing I've ever seen. Last night, I even curled up onto the floor right next to him, there in the kitchen. My back,' he says, placing an open palm on his coccyx.

We've stopped walking again. The sudden gravity of the conversation seems to require it. This is when he cries, still looking at me, thinning his lips and shrugging helplessly. I'm not good at public displays of emotion, especially with someone I've never met before. But the situation calls out for compassion, and I do have that. I reach out my hand and put it on his shoulder, and squeeze. I'm aware that I don't know his name, but then this isn't unusual among walkers, who are far more likely to know the names of dogs than they are their owners.

'I'm so sorry,' he says, trying to laugh it off, and I tell him he has nothing to apologise for. He looks up. 'The rain's not letting up, is it?'

'Best be getting home, no?'

He tries to smile. 'Good idea. And, look, thanks. Thanks for, you know, for listening. See you.'

But I do not see him again. Where does he go? Does he start walking the dog at a different time of day? Is he perhaps trying to avoid me? Or has something else happened, something bad? Maybe it's good news, a reconciliation? I will think about this man many times over the next few years, always hopeful that his relationship did recover, and fearful that it didn't, that she ultimately got custody of Boomer, leaving him bereft and alone. The unanswered questions are frustrating. I like a completed narrative. But then as a dog walker you pass briefly in and out of one another's lives. Some you learn about more than others, and some hang around for longer and become part of your daily routine. Often, you never learn their names. And a number do simply disappear, off beyond the park's outer limits, where they vanish into the texture of normal life and proper pavements, leaving their plotlines dangling, forever incomplete.

At home, Missy has rainwater pouring from her undercarriage like an open tap. She shakes, spraying the walls. I quickly hunt down the nearest towel to dry her, but it's too late, she's off up the carpeted stairs to be reunited with the rest of the family, leaving a cartoon trail of pawprints in her wake. One of the concessions you make when getting a dog is to give up the very notion of being house proud. There are myriad sprays that claim to eradicate pets' mess with one simple squirt, removing stains like magic, ta da. But this is a lie, a barefaced deception to prey on the needs of those that require this magic most. They never work.

Carpet's fucked. It'll have to come up.

Two

The police have cordoned off a large area of the park, and so suddenly my daily stroll has become a crime scene. As many as twenty people have congregated in one corner, and beyond them stand several police officers in hi-vis jackets whose only duty right now comprises keeping a solitary newspaper photographer at bay. Missy looks up at me, confused, and I shrug my shoulders. The park is essentially sectioned in half. Beyond the cordon are a dozen policemen and women walking in a line, scouring the ground for evidence, or DNA, a murder weapon.

Nothing like this has ever happened here before, not on my watch. This is an uneventful neighbourhood park, a municipal green used by locals either to congregate in, or to walk through on their way into town towards the shops, the train station, and the various schools nearby. Litter tends to be the worst crime committed. About two acres in size, it's divided down the middle by a pedestrian path cast in perpetual shadows by eighteen trees on each side, thirty-six in total. The trees are very tall, solid and brown. I've no idea what kind they are, but they are deciduous, I think, because right now they have very few leaves. The local squirrels consider them their adventure playground.

On this side, half a dozen fellow dog walkers have found themselves similarly confined, and I can't help but feel I've become an extra in a TV drama. Dog walkers are always stumbling onto crime scenes, it seems. On television, this is invariably an exciting development, but in real life it isn't, it's dreadful. I recognise no one, but there is tentative mingling nevertheless, everyone fizzing with human curiosity while mindful of conveying respect. We speak in whispers. 'What happened?' someone asks. I shrug back. 'No idea.' We could ask one of the officers, but they look very tall and very serious, and entirely occupied. Even the dogs appear to have read the room, each keeping close by.

One man, walking a large boxer, strolls gingerly past the congregated mourners, a group of people who have already transformed this stretch of railings into a shrine. They've placed bunches of flowers, dozens of them, and some blue helium balloons that bounce and sway in the breeze. The man with the boxer approaches the nearest policeman.

'What's happened, then?'

'A murder.'

'*A murder? Here?*'

The officer nods.

'When?'

'Last night.'

The man blanches, then retreats, and each of us reaches immediately for our phones. I find the news item quickly. 'A murder probe has been launched after a young man was stabbed to death opposite a park in—,' it reads. 'The victim in his twenties was found in the tree-lined street at about 10.20 p.m. on Thursday. Police, paramedics and air ambulance all attended, but despite their best efforts, the male died at the scene, which overlooks a nearby gastropub.' In a curious non sequitur, the item goes on to say that houses on 'the leafy road' fetch well in excess of one million, then adds that witnesses described how pub staff tried to save the young man's life when he staggered inside seeking help.

A hollow sensation settles in my stomach. I look towards the mourners, young men with their hoods up, the occasional woman. Several are crying propulsively. A woman with a Jack Russell glances over at me, tears collecting in her own eyes, and she says to me, 'Awful, just awful.' She hurries away. I turn back too, suddenly wanting to see my wife, my daughters, and I clip the dog to the lead.

They say that dogs have no real concept of time, but Missy's own internal clock is now sounding its silent alarm. 'Too soon,' her expression reads. Steadying herself on her front legs, she very deliberately lowers her rear to the ground and sits, refusing to move. The look she gives me would be discernible in any language: *No*. Over the next few years, this will become an increasingly regular situation we face: stalemate between creatures of opposing views. No matter how long or short the walk, or how bored she seems during it, she decides that it is always too soon to return home. Being a comparatively small dog, I am at least stronger than her. But stubbornness is the heaviest temperament, and she's a deadweight. Now, the lead tightens between us, and I begin to pull. Her face is impassive, pink tongue protruding. 'Oh, come on,' I plead. She rolls her shoulders once in response, firming her stance. Just beyond my line of vision, I sense some of the mourners watching this tug-of-war. I'm painfully aware that this is neither the time nor the place. '*Please*,' I tell her. But the more I pull, the more she squares herself, her centre of gravity low and sure. I tempt her with a treat, but she's not an idiot. I pull again, and her neck stretches and elongates, as if impersonating a giraffe.

'Good luck,' says the man with the boxer. 'Looks like he's not going anywhere.'

'*She*,' I say, correcting him.

It's only at the point when her neck now seems longer than I've ever seen it, practically elastic, that she gives in and begins dutifully to trot alongside me. Nothing in her demeanour suggests capitulation, or lingering annoyance. She has simply changed her mind, and the stand-off is forgotten already, a thing of the past, the canine memory bank immediately reset to *right now*. With her moist snout, she taps my shin twice to inform me that the treat I'd offered before, the one she'd ignored? Well, she'll accept it now.

Up ahead, I spy Wilson on one of his effortful power-walks, the poodle he'd only agreed to get in the first place to pacify his wife and family bouncing puppyishly behind him and desperately seeking other dogs to annoy. Wilson is not a dog person. Neither is he much of a people person. He'd given in to the repeated pleadings for a dog on the strict condition that it would be a small one, but Coco has continued to grow on telescopic legs, and is now level with his waist. This hasn't pleased him, but it has given him more fuel. Wilson is happiest when displeased, when he has something to direct his otherwise nameless anger towards. He is a middle-aged man for whom life has become an ongoing battle, one he secretly believes he is steadily losing. Everything bothers him: tax hikes, bicycle lanes, rising immigration, pack mentality. He doesn't like politicians or oat milk, and once he told me that he was deeply suspicious of men who wear shoes without socks. He is opposed on principle to the congestion charge. Driving his car into the city and not paying it constituted, for him, a *win*. In court, his lawyer cited diminished responsibility, and he was given six months to pay both the multiple charges he'd racked up and the accompanying fine.

I learned over time to avoid Wilson. In literal terms, I no longer have the energy for him. He's someone I knew before dogs. Our children had attended the same school. Back then, each conversation we had felt like I was interrupting a private argument that had been taking place in his head before spilling out into the open. He did not appreciate my efforts at amelioration. Once the primary school years were over, we drifted apart in the way that men tend easily to do. The requirement to know one another was no longer there, and this, I think, was a shared relief. Today, he knows that I have seen him, and I know that he has seen me, but both of us appear perfectly content to pretend otherwise, heads down.

One of the more intriguing things that I've recognised about myself recently – though Elena would call it concerning – is that social skills are like muscles: if you don't use them, they atrophy, they waste away. While I've been pleasantly relieved to learn that I can still talk to strangers in the park, and engage with them – as long as they come bearing a dog of their own – I've lost the ability to do so with anyone else for the simple sake of it, old acquaintances like Wilson included. I no longer need small talk. The friendships I had in my teens and twenties, which I nurtured well into my thirties and beyond, have drifted mostly because I allowed them to. And whenever I got back in touch, I learned that they too had allowed other friendships to drift. 'It's what we do,' Pavlov would tell me, adding, to remove ambiguity, 'men, I mean.'

The last time I was properly socially active was during the girls' primary school years, where school-gate inter-action was a requirement. There were summer barbecues and Christmas drinks with these strangers who had recently become friends, or at least friendly, and talk revolved around sport, and house prices, and holiday plans, and rarely went any deeper. They were the kind of conversations that could be readily interrupted because one of the children had tripped over, or lost their ball, or went suddenly and dramatically into anaphylactic shock, after which everyone was simply too tired to pick up the lost thread. They were friendships born out of convenience, and I appreciated them for what they were.

But, a while ago, without really noticing it, I think I must have decided that I'd met enough people in life already, and had had all my close friendships. I was good at friendship once. A good listener, people would seek me out. I miss that, but I don't miss the accompanying drama. There was always so much accompanying drama.

Elena worries for me, on my behalf. She does not approve of my increasing solitude, and thinks it's damaging to exist within my own echo chamber. She argues that an exchange of ideas, and small talk too, is good for us, good for the soul. While I've retreated, she has gone out and established new social groups which she works hard at maintaining. She is a fully functioning member of the neighbourhood, and I admire her, and also envy her. But I also have no real desire to emulate her because I can't, not any more.

It came as something of a surprise, then, to both of us, that I now often return home from an afternoon's walk having lost all track of time in pursuit of occasionally profound conversations with complete strangers.

'See?' Elena often said, and I knew that she wasn't gloating but was instead relieved, taking this as confirmation that, at some level, her husband still functioned, and hadn't been entirely consumed by age and gender stereotype just yet.

She would always express surprise at the stories I came back with, all this new information I had so abruptly gleaned. 'When I walk the dog,' she says, 'that's all I do: I walk the dog.' *Her* dog walking conversations rarely get particularly personal, and talk revolves around school and children. 'But I don't learn where they grew up, or why they were in hospital last week, or the precise reasons why they've been signed off work with anxiety for the past few months. How do *you* do it?' she asks. She doesn't wait for an answer. 'You know, I'm convinced it's done you the world of good.'

In truth, I've no idea how it's happened. I surprise myself. Since we've had the dog, windows have opened into new worlds. When I got ill, I was told to slow down. 'This may be your problem,' one of many doctors told me. 'You never did slow down, you just kept going.' I was told that I didn't relax, that I didn't approach meditation with the correct mindset, and that time away from work and screens would be good for me. 'Your body's trying to tell you something. Learn to listen.' I never did fully stop, because I never wanted to. I put family first, and work, and decided that everything else I could live without. I let certain friendships drift after becoming a parent, and ill-health only enhances the disconnect. I stopped going out, and focused all my efforts on managing my diminished energy levels, and how to exist on what remained. I'd often read that men of a certain age cleave towards isolation anyway; at least now I had an excuse.

I never saw Missy as a therapy aid, not at first. But this

is what she became. For Elena, a burden has been lifted. She can send me out now, knowing I'll be fine. In the park, I don't actively seek out anyone's company, but I find it nevertheless. And I certainly don't ask intrusive questions; rather, the conversation just seems to flow, and I'm reminded that I used to be good at this. The more meandering the walk, the more rambling the talk.

But context plays its part here, too. Elena walks the dog in the morning, when she is pushed for time. The people she meets are on a similarly tight schedule: the office looms, the commute and the working day. No one here has time to dawdle.

But the mid-afternoon shift are a different breed. We are people who are plugging a gap that needs to be filled, and so we bring with us another disposition. There are no early-morning frowns, but rather more open expressions: amblers keen to connect. Each of us has the luxury of time. We are either unemployed, or underemployed, or, worse, *freelance*, and we are trying to fill up the endless parcels of time that make up a typical day. If the morning tends to fly by, then there are a disproportionate number of hours in the afternoon. Dinner always seems ages away. We've been alone since breakfast, and we're hungry for diversion.

The word I hear most here between the hours of three and 4.30 p.m. is, 'Hi!', the exclamation mark practically visible.

An official murder investigation is launched the following day into the park death. No one will be convicted for the crime. Over the coming months, the helium evaporates and the balloons deflate, but the flowers remain. At first they're replenished every few days, placed alongside bottles whose labels read Cream Deluxe and which, Pavlov explains, after having looked it up online one afternoon, is the 'lightest and fastest premium cream charger on the planet', a sentence whose meaning manages to elude both of us entirely. A charger? For the next week or so, mourners arrive to coincide with my daily walk, long after the police tape is taken down. Cars pull up, BMWs and small Fords with go-faster stripes, parking bullishly on double yellow lines, and disgorging yet more people wanting to pay their respects. I watch as one person arrives with a bottle of Luc Belaire Rosé, which he opens and pours ceremoniously onto the grass in front of the flower display, and the weight of his heartache is so palpable I'm surprised his knees don't buckle. I watch as traffic wardens congregate like crows, seeing the crowd but also clocking their illegally parked cars, then wrestling with the dilemma of what to do, and when to do it. One of the mourners approaches them, frowning.

'Have some respect, mate,' he says. The warden nervously retreats.

Missy observes all this with a concern so intent I half wonder whether she might be taking notes. While she is normally happy to sniff every blade of grass in this park at least twice, she always endeavours to give the mourners and their small rectangle of ceremonial earth a wide berth, as if instinctively aware that a certain decorum is required here, a dog in tune with human sensitivity at the very moment she most needs to be.

Does this mean she is picking up on *my* needs too? Elena was right. I had been cocooning myself in, trapped by poor health within the four walls of home, like one of those pigeons that fly into a shopping mall and can't find their way out again, condemned to panic-flutter from floor to floor against the backdrop of never-changing scenery. Sometimes I wonder how I didn't go mad, and then fear that perhaps I did and don't realise it, unaware-ness being a condition, a by-product, of my new state. Either way, I'm back out in the world again now, in increments admittedly, and counting my footsteps, but I'm out nevertheless, with this new companion of mine who surprises me daily by following me dutifully, as if I were the master in this set-up, and not the servant. I admit that it felt strange at first, and almost alien – I had never owned one before – but now we are man and dog, a familiar sight, part of the local landscape.

'Progress,' Elena says.

Three

My first official sighting of Lintang comes when I'm circling the park one afternoon with Pavlov and Elizabeth. I'm fairly established here by now, Missy four years old, and part of the pack. We're walking together on this bright, brisk day, a wind whipping in from somewhere cruel, the sky streaked with the acne scars of broken cloud cover, when we hear a commotion over by the fire exit, and see three small dogs, Pomeranians, so dainty, primped and fluffed, that they are surely the creation of a gluten-free patisserie chef. Each is becoming increasingly tangled within their respective leads and so they quickly come to resemble a Hydra-headed snake. Meanwhile, a woman is attempting to thread them one by one through the turnstile that everyone else tends to avoid because of its creaking weight.

The dogs' barks are shrill and impatient, and the walker looks cowed and nervous. Once she's eventually in, she keeps them on their leads but doesn't walk any further in, instead hovering expectantly as if waiting for them to do their business quickly and efficiently so that she can turn and leave again. They don't. Instead they dawdle, and turn in small circles, intermittently looking up at the woman as if to say, 'What now?' The woman is tiny, dressed in a purple Puffa jacket, stonewashed jeans and chunky no-brand ankle-high trainers. Even from this distance I can see that she radiates an awkwardness that conveys this isn't her natural terrain, that she isn't supposed to be here, and that she is far from happy.

'My guess,' Pavlov says, 'is her first time. Also, they are not her dogs.'

I ask him why.

'Because. Because look at her. She doesn't know what to do. She waits for them to make shit, but this is not how you make your dog shit.'

So much of my conversation with Pavlov revolves around faeces. His dog, Dog, has a complicated digestive system, a saga he has recounted to me on more than one occasion.

'Come,' he says, 'we go help.'

This suggestion is less an example of his instinctive philanthropy towards others, and more an illustration of his need to insert himself into everything that takes place within these confines. Dog, for one, is always happy with his owner's reluctance to return home in quick time. A

32

grizzled Staffordshire terrier, Dog has one ear, three legs, and a surprisingly amenable disposition. He also slobbers in a manner that ensures I always keep him at arm's length. He is partially deaf, and so Pavlov has to shout a lot, but like all dogs' presumed deafness, his is mostly selective. He spends a lot of his time here circumnavigating the park's bins, because there are always treasures to be found at the foot of the bins. He and Pavlov may have a deep connection, but every dog needs its space. They are cooped up together in a small flat for much of every day, and so the park, when they get here, is nature in all its splendour.

Pavlov, meanwhile, nods to everyone in both his immediate and peripheral vision. He likes to know your business, but is happier still recounting *his* to everyone else. I have already heard a great many chapters of his life story, this figurative memoir he adds to daily with myriad asides that sometimes stretch credulity, and would, I feel, likely buckle under the weight of fact checking. He is incorrigible, and sometimes he is a bit much, but he is also difficult to dislike.

'I think we just leave her be,' Elizabeth counters. Elizabeth is seventy-nine years old, and, like her dog Betty, is a fundamentally gentle soul whose presence has the calming air of a scented candle. She listens more than she talks, but she does so with clear interest, her blue eyes sparkling. She is everyone's ideal grandmother figure, and over the years I have come to feel incredibly fond of her.

'She'll work it out herself,' Elizabeth says.

'Elizabeth,' Pavlov counters, her name in his mouth

like a dropped stone. 'We are a community here, we help each other, no? This woman, she needs our help. Or at least her dogs do. So, we help. Come.'

As we approach, the Pomeranians assume the behaviour of cats. They watch us and the dogs draw near, and they arch their backs. Their bright ginger fur begins to shiver, and they peel back black lips to reveal pink gums and white teeth. They circle one another, moving both forwards and backwards, and in doing so tangle themselves up again. Above them, the woman looks close to tears.

'Hello, hello!' Pavlov says. 'We help.' He instructs the woman to let go of the leads. 'Let them go, drop!' He then picks up one of the dogs, and hands it to me. It weighs less than a club sandwich. He gives another to the woman, and takes the remaining one for himself. For their part, the dogs seem entirely content to be handled, and in fact appear to prefer being cradled in arms than on the damp grass. Their cold black eyes bulge like marbles.

'Now,' Pavlov says, 'you walk this way, *you* walk over there, I step back. The leads will follow us, this I promise. Okay, do it.'

Slowly but steadily the dogs become free. Pavlov beams.

'Now,' he says. 'Now we let the dogs go,' and as he says this, he unclips each of them while the woman's own eyes grow wide in italicised alarm. 'To do their business, yes?'

'*Wait!*' she cries. 'They won't come back!'

The dogs scurry away on matchstick legs, a high-kicking running style that looks both ridiculous and rather touching, a canine *Swan Lake*. Pavlov, who is in his early sixties and has a certain bearing to him, reassures the woman. 'They will return, trust me. And if not? We make chase!'

He ascertains that this is indeed her first time walking them, and that, no, they do not belong to her but rather to her employer. Her voice is meek, little more than an accented whisper, and she doesn't make eye contact. She peers up at him with an expression somewhere between confusion and awe, as if she isn't used to people talking to her quite so openly. He introduces himself, and then us – Elizabeth smiles with warmth – and now he asks her name, which is Lintang, and where she is from, and she says Indonesia. She offers nothing else. An anxious frown settles across her forehead, tramlines awaiting their train.

'The dogs,' she says. 'I must go.'

The Pomeranians have flocked back to her. They form a triangle by her feet, bums facing in, trembling snouts out, and they shit in companionable unison, three tiny deposits that elicit precious little interest from Dog, who is otherwise normally fascinated by the excretion of his peers. The woman, Lintang, frowns, and swallows hard, and then searches in her pockets for poo bags. Pavlov watches on with amused interest. She collects the deposits while pulling the face of someone whose life can surely sink no lower, and holds her breath until she reaches the bin, grateful to relinquish the bags into its circular maw.

As she re-harnesses them, each barks once, as if issuing

instruction, or approval. She looks up at us and nods in what might be either a thank you or simple acknowledgement, and then retreats to tackle the turnstile gate while her cheeks burn a crimson red.

'Bye bye,' she says.

Over the next few weeks and months, each of us will grow increasingly concerned about Lintang, about how she is living and the manner in which she is being *kept*. But not yet. Now, she is simply a curiosity about whom Pavlov, at least, craves to know more.

'Hm,' he murmurs. 'There is something not quite right here, I think.'

It was long ago established in our friendship that I am his prompt, the one to encourage him to talk more. 'What do you mean?' I ask.

'I don't know. But something about her. It rings wrong bell, you know? Not ding dong, but dong dong.'

Pavlov was born in Russia, but left before his eighteenth birthday. His accent has mostly lost its crunchy consonants and serrated vowel sounds, but these he nevertheless occasionally deploys for effect, as he does his aphorisms, which he will sometimes drop into conversations convinced of their charm. In this, he isn't entirely wrong.

'She's scared,' he says. 'Not just of us, and her dogs, but of everyone and everything, you know? She is rabbit, and the world is headlights.'

'Poor thing,' Elizabeth says. 'Although,' she adds, beginning to smile, 'I'm not surprised she's afraid of *you*.'

Pavlov looks aghast. 'Me? Who can be scared of me?' He shrugs. 'Okay, for sure, because of this head, perhaps.'

He points to his shaved skull, with its nicks and scars, the occasional dent. 'But she was also scared of you, Elizabeth, and who could ever be afraid of a great lady such as you?'

'Oh, give over,' she says, laughing.

I'd been the newcomer to this established group, the only one with a puppy, and even now I still feel a little uncertain as to my role here, self-consciously aware that my intermittent presence amongst them might have come between Pavlov and Elizabeth and, in a way, divided them. While they're the park's veterans, and are occasionally joined by several others of a similar vintage, I had only dipped in and out of their circle for the first few years, combining my daily walk with post-school playground duty, where my focus was my children, not people either approaching, or well into, retirement age. I'd see them regularly for the simple reason that they were always here, and felt as drawn to them as I was to their dogs who, like them, were also getting on a bit, greying around the muzzle, and beginning to slow down. Dog and Betty had known each other since they were rescued as youngsters. They share very few physical similarities – one squat and overweight, and hobbling; the other tall and elegant, with an almost equine canter to her walk – but they have between them the enviable ease of siblings who enjoy a deep mutual affection. Missy herself was particularly fond of them too, and spent a disproportionate amount of her youth trying desperately to lick the gums of an unaccountably patient Dog whenever she saw him. Pavlov explained that this was due to Dog's maternal bearing, this despite the continued presence of his testicles. From what Pavlov has told me, he and Elizabeth had fallen into a surprisingly easy friendship almost immediately, two people who, on paper, have very little in common outside of their love of dogs – one a Russian immigrant, the other a quiet widow – but who fit well together simply because they are both at the stage in life where they appreciate being able to rely upon some recurrent and easy company. They discuss art, politics, literature, the weather; they talk about their dogs. Pavlov admits that he does most of the talking.

'But only because she likes to listen,' he insists, 'and because I am interesting!'

When I first arrived on the scene, and onto their patch, Pavlov had viewed me as fresh meat, a new set of ears to listen to an old set of stories already familiar to his walking partner. 'We don't have desks to get back to any more,' Pavlov told me. 'No more bosses. Come, join us.'

I'd fallen in with them on that day – Missy a tiny puppy – and listened, with Elizabeth, as Pavlov, having ascertained my new status as dog owner, told me what to expect, how to behave, how to conduct myself, 'and to not look so nervous when strangers approach you to talk. I don't bite, you know,' he said, adding, 'and neither does he,' and pointed to his dog. Pavlov is a man who requires an audience, and here he has a captive one. Occasionally, I marvel at Elizabeth's patience, but several months into our acquaintance I spy a very small set of hearing aids nestling deep within her earlobes, and I wonder whether I might have discovered the source of their lasting friendship. Hearing aids have a volume control.

Together, they have walked into a thousand urban sunsets.

Pavlov is single, and has been for many years. 'There comes a time,' he says, 'when you cannot share your home with anyone else, not any longer. You develop habits, you see? You need your own space, where you can be you and no one can say one damn thing about it.'

To this, Elizabeth snorts, but Pavlov can sometimes choose not to hear, too.

He told me that his mother had escaped communist Russia back in the 1970s, and when he told me this story for a second time, several months later, the 1970s had become the 1980s. A new life here was difficult for his mother, he said, who went on to suffer lengthy bouts of depression prompted, he felt, by a sense of alienation in an adopted country that didn't always look kindly upon immigrants. He learned the language quickly but kept his accent as a badge of honour. He struggled at school.

'School is waste of time for me, you know? I teach myself everything I need to know. University of life, yes? Is cliché, but true-true.'

In his early twenties, he ran a market stall in a fashionable part of town, or at the very least he worked on one at weekends. He became the acquaintance of certain luminaries, he claimed: Vivienne Westwood and Joe Strummer; Peter Fonda and Timothy Leary. He had travelled widely, and spoke lustily about the women he had loved, and who had tempted him into their respective lairs: San Francisco to Singapore, and, once, Selhurst

Park, near Crystal Palace, where, he confided, the love of his life died.

'The *love* died, you understand. Not the woman, she didn't die. She went on to marry dentist who drove Vauxhall Astra. They have a timeshare in Algarve now. Pity.'

I had met people like Pavlov before, of course. They tended to be famous or infamous, occasionally both, and lived in a world in which they were the centre of their own universe. Others were fated to orbit them, and people like me, a journalist, were sent to interview them, thereby allowing them to bask in the ongoing conviction of their own importance, like beached seals in the sun. I used to think that only high achievers were like this, and possessed of this particular mindset, but Pavlov has proved otherwise. The product of difficult circumstances, he had not lived the life he might once have envisaged for himself, but his confidence hadn't entirely died, and when he found the appropriate audience – which, on a midweek afternoon, was me – that confidence took full flight with an impressive wingspan.

Pavlov walked with a pronounced limp, the result of a car accident, he told me; after which, despite the medical care, there had been complications and his bones failed to heal properly.

'Hospital for six months, and so much pain. So much time in bed, in cold, cold ward. The things I see there; such things that happened to me.'

His leg has worsened over the years, and now, at sixty or so, the grinding bones of his joints have left him in permanent pain. His hip knows when it's going to rain before he does. After quickly building up a tolerance for painkillers, and living in a country where OxyContin was not readily available, he turned instead to alcohol.

'But drugs I have done, of course,' he says. 'All of them, for experiment. Amphetamine is my favourite.'

He boasts of having had minor skirmishes with the law, one of which resulted in a four-week prison term which he continues to maintain was a 'misunderstanding'. In his thirties, he managed to buy his own flat, but after a recession, was left in negative equity for decades.

'And now the bank extends me no more credit, they don't want to know. A black mark on my name, unfair.'

He lives these days in a one-bedroom council house on an estate that has been slated for demolition, at which point he will be rehoused elsewhere. But, Pavlov tells me, a vein throbbing the length of his forehead, 'they will carry me out in coffin, I am going nowhere.'

He used to work as a cartoonist for a political magazine, and then as a graphic designer. But most of that work evaporated years ago, as he became increasingly prehistoric in the modern era. 'Adobe Illustrator, I have no idea of. No interest. QuarkXPress? No thank you.' He takes the occasional commission for niche websites that pay poorly but which, if nothing else, keep him occupied and give him something to complain about. Due to both his and Dog's increasingly limited mobility – Dog walks just fine on three legs, but tires easily – their horizons have closed in. The world for them now extends no further than this park and the Co-op they pass en route. Both live on packet noodles, tinned food and Monster Munch. Pavlov has told me that he could do with a visit to the dentist, 'but I don't trust dentists, so.'

Though he puts on a brave face, I can see his suffering. It's all there in his surface anger, his multiplying frustrations. The majority of his remaining positivity is poured into Dog. He loves all dogs, he tells me, and often becomes tearful talking about them. If he has seen enough of humankind to last him whatever remains of his lifetime, then for animals he has nothing but continued respect. Without Dog knowing, he feeds the neighbour's cat, and leaves out dishes of food in the alleyway opposite his flat for the night-time foxes. He speaks to Keith about cockatoos, and he once spent an involving hour telling me about the mating habits of elephants.

If he sees someone here being aggressive towards their dog, he intervenes. His one extravagance is the purchasing of cheap canine treats, and these he brings with him to hand out with a Pied Piper generosity. Missy adores him unreservedly.

Pavlov is not the sort of person to disappear easily into a crowd. He is tall and stocky, broad-shouldered and square-chinned, his once-muscular form now converted into an ageing bulk which will soon melt towards fat. Catch him in a certain light, shadows falling just so, and you'll see a hint of Frankenstein's monster. He owns a limited wardrobe. In the summer, he wears a tight black T-shirt, black jeans within which his legs look like Bavarian sausages, and steel-capped boots. During colder temperatures, autumn and winter, he puts on a battered army jacket with a fleece of white wool at the collar. He is mostly bald, but the strands that remain at the back he grows long and binds together in a ponytail. In particularly cold months, he wears a black woollen hat pulled down low, and tucks the ponytail up inside it for 'protection'. Though he remains convinced the damage to the ozone layer has been exaggerated by a media pursuing its own agenda, he bears the scar on his scalp of an excised lesion, which he tells with a certain pride was skin cancer, caught early.

His interests are wide, if not particularly committed: men's football, women's football, the Iran/Iraq conflict, Israel versus Palestine. Millennials appal him. He will talk happily on any given subject, though he proffers most of them himself. But for all his commitment, many of his well-honed opinions are in danger of collapsing at the slightest inquisition. I've learned simply to let him talk, because talking is when he is happiest. I can't help but imagine him at home alone, silent and passive, reading something in the newspaper or seeing something on the television and wanting desperately to engage with someone about it, then turning around and seeing no one, just a permanently snoozing dog. And so if he doesn't come to life here in the park, then where? Very often, he keeps me talking for longer than I'd like, insisting on one more lap, then another still. In order for me to escape, either because I'm tired or have to make dinner for the girls, or simply because I've had enough for one day, I find myself reasoning with him in the only way that might make him let me go: by inventing a nagging sitcom wife who was expecting me home half an hour ago.

'Women! They are death of us, yes?' he grins. 'But you go. *Go.* Tomorrow again, yes?'

Relieved to be back home, I revert to type. I update

myself on the girls' movements, how their day at school went, and then I return to my office to finish work and answer emails. I wonder again about trying to write that book I've been vaguely planning, on and off, for years, before realising that I can't decide upon which font to use, and so I check my socials instead. I make dinner for myself and the girls, and keep Elena's plate warm for later. I fill the dishwasher, then go about picking up stray socks and hairbands in a house littered with stray socks and hairbands, and I turn off all the lights the girls have left on. I tie a knot in the recycling bag, and mean to take it to the bin outside but forget and leave it on the side instead, where it festers and sweats, its continued presence later prompting a by now familiar spousal confrontation. At some point, Elena comes rushing back from work, kisses everyone on proffered cheeks, then grabs her bike and heads off for the gym, telling me she'll eat later. I make a half-hearted attempt to encourage the girls into the living room to watch something together before remembering which century we are in, and they instead peel away to their respective rooms with their phones, leaving me to take up my place on the sofa where I switch on the television and settle on whatever lulls me into a stupefied trance in the shortest possible time. Alone but not quite, because the dog is with me, beached across my lap, where incrementally over the next couple of hours she rotates like a rotisserie chicken until she has settled on her back, between my thighs, mottled belly exposed, her four legs throwing semaphores into the space above her. Her tongue is lolling, and the heavy breathing will soon graduate into snores. Intermittently, she will twitch limbs in dreams, and silently she will fart a gas so noxious that I am at once affronted and also a little impressed. These are how my days mostly end, now.

And I still find myself peering down in a kind of ongoing bemusement at her very existence, the undeniable reality of her here in my house and on my lap, this thing that has come to dominate so much else so unambiguously, and who has transformed me into something I never thought I'd be in this life: a dog owner.

Four

I am a cat person. Having grown up on the ninth floor of a block of flats where the only dogs I'd encounter were the kind that had been trained to fight in the back room of pubs, a cat had been the only realistic option. There was Tom, and then Ben, both black and white and beautiful, but whose lives were fated to be short. Tom had been born with a flu so severe that we spent eighteen months tending to his streaming nostrils and weeping eyes before multiple organ failure ultimately did for him, while Ben, who couldn't be persuaded *not* to sit on the outside windowsill in a bullish defiance of vertigo, one day took a misstep, and fell. We swore off cats after that, convinced of a lurking bad luck, but then my mother was gifted a third, this one a Siamese who lived up to stereotype with a personality of such terrifying disdain that we became convinced he considered us beneath him. He spent most of the daylight hours hiding under the sofa, and eventually went on hunger strike. He was soon rehomed.

My final attempt at cat ownership, which began at the age of nineteen, endured two decades. Something about my mother seemed to encourage cats being given to her, and this one was another unasked-for gift. She arrived, the cat, just as I was preparing to leave home, and perhaps *because* I was leaving home, a concerned friend worried that my absence needed swiftly to be compensated for, and what better than a dependent kitten?

My mother named her Chelsea after a character in a film who, when I checked to confirm several months into her life, had actually been called Madison, by which time it was too late. Chelsea was my only consistent dependant during my single years. We were inseparable. We shared food, and a single bed, and on those few occasions when a new girlfriend shared it too, things got cramped. She was instinctively untrusting of strangers, but then how could she not be? She rarely interacted with anyone else. I did not, back then, have the means of living anywhere with outside space, and so her only contact with the wider world was restricted to a succession of window ledges and flat roofs, where she'd bask in the sunlight and sniff the currents on the air. Much of our shared relationship was based around my guilt. If I couldn't give her the spacious balconies or open lawns I imagine she craved, then I'd make sure she had anything else she could want.

When one girlfriend moved in and brought with her a
life-sized cardboard cut-out of the nineties pop star Seal,
explaining that it had been a birthday present from friends
she'd grown attached to, Chelsea was not happy. She
went to great pains to avoid it, pressing herself up against
the far wall, as if convinced that the singer who had found
fame with a song called 'Killer' might attack. During an
emotional outburst in part prompted by a few grams of
catnip, she one day pounced on it, claws out, and in doing
so caused irreparable damage to Seal's open-toed sandals.
My girlfriend failed to see the funny side. The relationship
never recovered.

A year later, during a subsequent date at home that
seemed to be going unaccountably well, I moved things
from the dinner table to the sofa, taking the bottle of
wine with us. The cat came too. As we settled back to
watch a film, Chelsea took up her usual proprietary place
on my lap and, after some silent consideration, extended
a paw which she rested upon my girlfriend's thigh. I took
this for what it plainly was, approval, and so I ultimately
did the only thing I could do after that: I married her.*

Chelsea lived for nineteen years. I have always hoped
that I gave her a full and stimulating life; I certainly gave
her love. At fifteen, she finally moved into a house, along
with me and a heavily pregnant Elena. The house came
with a small garden, a novelty for us, but by this time
she was set in her ways and mistrustful of the outdoors.

* The girlfriend, not the cat.

Despite encouragement, she remained inside, content with another novelty: three floors, and an actual staircase whose carpet she could unstitch, fibre yarn by fibre yarn, with claws still as sharp as needles. It seemed like she had little idea what to do with all this room now that, quite literally, we did have the space to swing a cat. But then she was old, and had grown if not quite fat then undeniably stout, and so lazing had become her natural state. She liked to wallow in the bathroom sink, and on an open ironing board, spreading her bulk like butter across its pointed tip. She felt settled here, and comfortable. She had borne all the many changes we'd gone through together with dignity and stoicism.

But this all changed towards the end of the pregnancy. The more it showed, the more she came to avoid Elena, much as she had once done with the cardboard pop star. In doing so, she reverted to her youthful behaviour by becoming my cat alone. She would sit with me in my office upstairs in the spare bedroom, slightly to the left of the keyboard, always on top of the sheets of paper I needed most. I typed to the sound of her lugubrious purr. When I went downstairs for lunch, she would follow, sitting on the table opposite my plate and sharing my food only when I gave her the nod. Chelsea had always been affectionate, and Elena would often come into the kitchen to see us pressing our noses together in a scene that, in another context, might have been misconstrued.

But then she began to retreat from me, too. At some point between Christmas and New Year 2005, we returned from the hospital to the house we had only just moved into three weeks previously, now with a baby in tow. Elena had been on the maternity ward for several days, and I'd been hoping they'd be happy to see one another again. Instead, the cat refused to come downstairs, and was soon exiting any room we entered. Efforts to introduce the new member of the family failed repeatedly, and Elena, whose head and heart were full with the baby, both respected this distance and, I felt, tacitly maintained it. She had more important things to worry about. But me? I felt a wrench. Where was my cat, my other half? Why was she no longer sitting with me? Why did she not come when called, and why did I have to hunt in every room before finding her hidden, curled up in corners, behind the sofa, or under the bed? She was absenting herself by stealth, and nothing I could do would bring her back into the fold.

It soon became obvious that she was ill, and steadily she lost weight. She'd creep about the house keeping close to the skirting boards, and I struggled to recognise her. Her features grew pointed, her teeth brown. Once I had needed two hands to heft her up; now, when I could catch her, I could scoop her up easily in one. The vet put her on a course of antibiotics, and she did rally but only briefly. I took her back, and the vet now offered X-rays, and mentioned the possibility of investigative surgery at an exorbitant cost. But she also reminded me that Chelsea was old, and that nineteen was a good innings. She suggested that perhaps we could let nature take its course.

'With these pills,' she said, 'she won't be in pain. But don't leave it too long. Come back to me when you think it's *time*.'

I made a bed up for her in the kitchen. Her weight loss was drastic. I picked her up gently, and put her by her bowl, encouraging her to eat, not the usual tinned stuff or its dried equivalent but some slow-boiled chicken soft enough to melt in the mouth. She resisted. She resisted the water, too. I picked her back up, cradling her in my palms, and placed her back onto the plump cushion.

'If you need anything,' I told her, 'I'll be upstairs. Come up and get me.'

I returned an hour later to find she hadn't moved. She eyed me impassively. I could not remember the last time I'd heard her purr. I stroked her gently, fingers tracing the xylophone of her spine, the harp strings of her ribs. I recalled how, years ago, the first time I exposed her to catnip, she pressed her ears flat to her skull while her eyes ballooned in their sockets, and she raced around the wooden floors of the flat with all the exaggerated calamity of a cartoon character, her claws trying to find purchase, the speed of her alarming and hysterical. She would return from her mad dash and press her nose into the pouch for another dose before, whoosh, she was off again, cresting the back of the sofa and the armchair, free-jumping from table to kitchen counter to the top of the fridge, then stopping suddenly to peer down at me, pupils like saucers. The same cat. The same cat as this, now. I stroked her again, and tried not to cry. A week ago, at the vet, I'd wondered how I would know when it was *time*.

I knew.

The following morning, Elena and I had an argument.

I don't remember what it was about now, but it was something small and trivial, a meaningless squabble in lieu of articulating all the many difficulties that had come with having a small baby, who by then was almost nine months old. Elena had just returned to work after maternity leave, following weeks of broken, sleepless nights, of hours pacing the bedroom, and all the rocking, soothing, feeding, and the still-novel realities of having to tiptoe about the place in order to maintain those precious few moments of peace and quiet whenever they did by chance occur. Life had blossomed out for us both into something entirely new, and which had to be learned. It had changed everything.

In a pattern that would come helplessly to define her, Elena was running late. The nursery was conveniently located within the grounds of her workplace, but dropping off was always a protracted exercise, and could only add to that lateness. There was no time for breakfast, just the manic back and forth in the midst of a frazzled atmosphere both of us still hoped was merely temporary. We raised our voices at one another for a bit, and then she heaved the pushchair out, not quite slamming the front door behind her but closing it hard enough for it to rattle. Their absence brought an immediate peace, within which I felt both relief and a lurking guilt.

Still in the kitchen, on her bed next to the radiator, Chelsea hadn't moved. Her food remained untouched. The situation now seemed grave. When I attempted to pick her up, various parts of her collapsed around my fingers. She was alive, and looking at me intently, but was barely sentient. A heavy pressure settled on my chest

52

as, now dressed, I carried the cat in my arms on a stumbling ten-minute walk to the vet. I had not called ahead as it hadn't dawned on me to do so – hadn't even called, or consulted with, Elena – but Chelsea seemed to be suffering now, and I couldn't bear that, needing simply to get there as quickly as I could. This I explained in a rush to the receptionist who, with a sad smile, encouraged me to take a seat and to wait, indicating that I'd be called in shortly.

The vet was businesslike, brisk. 'It *is* time,' she confirmed. I looked at her green uniform, covered with so much fur from so many animals. 'It's right that you brought her in now. I'll give you a moment.'

The room hung heavy with a thousand ghosts, their lingering scent draped around the room like curtains. Chelsea was tiny on the table. I stroked her gently, and pressed my nose to hers, which was no longer moist but rather dry and cold. I told her over and over again how sorry I was, that I loved her, that she was my cat, and I'd never forget her, and that I hoped I'd done well by her, as well as I could in the circumstances. She gazed dutifully up at me, but the light in her eyes, nineteen years there, was gone.

The vet came back in. She explained about the injection. 'It'll be painless,' she said, 'and she'll fall into a deep sleep, and then . . .'

She asked whether I wanted to stay for the end, adding quickly that many people choose not to, that they preferred to say goodbye, and then leave. 'It will be entirely painless, I promise you. She's just going to sleep.'

I had no idea what to do, and my prevarication was

costing the vet valuable time. She placed her hand on
mine and said, 'It's okay, it's okay.' I gave the cat a kiss,
a last kiss, and left quickly, eagerly even. Out on the
street, I was immediately drenched in remorse, convinced
now that I should have stayed despite the vet's assur-
ances, that I had abandoned her at the very end, and
how could I have done that? But I knew how: I did not
want to see my cat die. I did not want that.

The road ahead blurred through a prism of tears, the
colour of the traffic lights swam purple and pale. At
home, I called Elena and told her. Her shock took me
by surprise. She cried out, a purely instinctive scream
down the phone, and a single word. '*No.*' I pictured her
there in the office, her third day back after maternity
leave, wiping her cheeks, and becoming the focal point
of concerned colleagues.

'I'll call you later, yes?' she said.

The house felt enormous, it felt empty. I went upstairs,
and hesitated by the baby's room. I stood over the empty
cot. Slowly, I became aware of a sharp, tight smell, one
entirely familiar to new parents and pet owners alike. I
checked the soles of my shoes, and then, turning, spotted
in the far corner of the room by the cupboard a small,
neat shit, curled in the concentric shape of a 99 ice
cream. Cat shit. My first response was confusion, then
disbelief, but then came a curious sort of admiration. I
approached it, and my crime scene suspicions were
confirmed. This was a recent deposit.

Chelsea had not been upstairs in weeks. I'd been
convinced that she was no longer capable of it. She barely
walked, and when she did, was unsteady on her feet.

Often, she collapsed where she lay, simply falling back into a fitful sleep. As far as I knew, she'd never been in the baby's bedroom at all, and had always resisted it, as if convinced that this was the one room in this new house that contained within it a manifestation of evil. We both laughed at this in wonder, Elena and I, this deep dislike that she had felt for our daughter. But it also unsettled us. It upset me that something we had made together had put *her* out quite so much. The baby had made her miserable, but had this been the cause of her becoming ill, of hastening her demise?

How, then, had she pulled off this final dirty protest? The message was as emphatic as it was unambiguous. Was there any other way to read it? I marvelled at the effort it must have taken, the dogged determination, too. What a strange thing to do, so openly hostile, but also defiant and declarative. She had always been a cat that knew her own mind – is there any other kind? – and had unfailingly managed to communicate to me her feelings.

And now, at the very end, *this*.

Any dog would have a hard time following her.

The dog came like old hire-purchase payments: in instalments. She was a concept at first, and then a working theory. 'Yes, but if we get a dog, what if . . .?' There was all the usual discussion that takes place within a family: who would walk her, and how often? Which of us would clean up after her? Having never owned a dog before, there were many unknown unknowns. We asked around, searched the internet. There remained the lingering conviction that dogs were for other people, older people, those who had settled down. Dogs tied you to one place, and restricted your movements. I had not met many people in their twenties and thirties with dogs; instead, they came as an addendum to having had children in midlife. They were for people who favoured routine.

Which of course was the whole point. I was one of them now. I had two children of, according to online opinion, optimum dog-owning age (ten and eight), a house and a mortgage, a Netflix account, wine in the fridge. I didn't go out very much any more, rarely travelled, had become dependable and ordered. But still, we were reluctant to rush into things, and so got the girls some gerbils instead. These proved no substitute, however. The girls quickly grew bored, and within weeks resumed texting us pictures of puppies. Late-night conversations came to revolve almost exclusively around what was by now a collective longing that we nurtured for at least a year, maybe more, the gradual approach towards the inevitable tipping point. Elena thought it a good idea, and hesitantly but increasingly so did I. A dog was simply the next thing to check off on the to-do list of life.

The only thing that continued to give me pause was my health, this perpetual lack of energy that had slowed me down and which had forced me, unwillingly and far too early, into a pace of life I had previously thought was the preserve of the elderly. How could I possibly manage a dog? I'd spent the past several years playing guinea pig for a fleet of doctors whose interest in me had quickly waned the longer a concrete diagnosis remained elusive. I'd been passed from one to the other to be made sense of; to make dutiful note of the glandular fever when aged eighteen; the suspected avian flu at forty-two; the proliferation of further flus and colds in between and thereafter; in addition to the ongoing struggles of my mitochondrial cells that were clearly no longer working as they should. Successive treatments failed. I had blood tests and physicals, endoscopies and colonoscopies, X-rays, a barium test, an MRI. At one point, psycho-therapy was recommended. 'Because why not?' the doctor said. But he wasn't able to refer me on the National Health Service because the Q&A sheet he had asked me to fill out revealed that I didn't have depression. No depression equals no referral. So I went private. I found the therapy fascinating, but no firm conclusions were reached. Not that there was nothing there, but that there wasn't enough, the therapist told me, to explain a likely psychological cause for all *this*.

'Your ailments might well be more physical than they are anything else,' she said. 'And you're coping pretty well, I'd say.'

Nevertheless, digestive issues then manifested, requiring yet more X-rays. My diet shrank the more my intolerance to various foods increased, and I went nowhere without protein bars, just in case I got light-headed and began abruptly craving calories. I went to bed reliably hungry simply because I was never eating quite enough. I lost weight. The hospital became uncom-fortably familiar, and I stopped losing myself down its endless corridors because I knew my way around as well as any porter. During one of the later oscopies, which I'd been accurately forewarned would be long and painful, I was held down firmly in the foetal position by two muscular nurses to manage the convulsing and the bucking that would surely take place. While they chatted amiably about last night's football somewhere above me, I became aware of water leaking steadily from my eyes, not crying so much as simply all the accumulated sadness leaching out of me. Frequently, I was referred to other specialists on different waiting lists, but I never quite reached the front of the queue. The silence grew deafening.

Any dog that came into my life, then, would most likely have preferred the old me to the current model.

And then Billy arrived.

Billy was the most confident of the neighbourhood cats, ink black and ridiculously handsome with his amber eyes and alert ears. Except when fighting, he possessed the personality of a Buddhist monk, serene and calm and stately, and he proceeded to steal the family's hearts in the way that only a cat can.

He lived somewhere down the road, his owner unknown to us, and we first encountered him sitting on our garden wall on the way back from school one afternoon, as if patiently awaiting our return, an appointment we'd forgotten but he had not. Charmed by his brazenness, we opened the door and in he waltzed, into both the kitchen and our lives. He jumped up onto the dinner table and nodded once in my direction, giving me the permission to stroke him. He stayed for dinner.

Over the next many months, Elena repeated her misgivings. The cat wasn't ours. We were taking him from his rightful owners. Our counter-argument was that he returned whether we fed him or not. When I politely sent him on his way, he came back. It isn't easy banishing beauty from your home. The girls loved him. In time, he stayed the night, and was a regular face at breakfast. He liked the peanut butter we spread on toast.

We tracked down his owner, and explained the situation. The owner wasn't happy, but still Billy returned. When there were cat fights out in the street late at night, I stumbled out of bed to go rushing to save him. He didn't need my protection; this was his street, his rules. But he saw me, and appreciated my efforts nevertheless. He came sauntering over, curling his velvet form around my ankles, the girls in their pyjamas waiting at the door on their knees, arms open for an embrace he was always willing to grant.

Pleas for a dog fell silent, because for now we were sated.

I was a cat person, still.

Five

The second time I see Lintang, she emerges as if from nowhere to rush to my aid. At first there is nothing but the flashing of teeth and flying fur, and an increasing panic climbing high in my throat. But then I become aware, at the corner of my eye, of someone approaching at speed, her progress impeded by three small dogs that she has to step over and around while crying out, in a voice that rises to a plate-smashing shriek, 'Hey! Hey! *Hey!*'

By now, Missy is in my arms, and I'm lifting her as high as I can, as if she were a medal I'd just won and am holding aloft for the crowd to admire. Below us is another dog, also a Border, who has temporarily lost its mind and is leaping wildly and attempting to sink its teeth into one of Missy's dangling back legs.

This is Missy's first fight. I've heard about dogfights, they're notorious, a perennial hot topic of conversation in the park: how they can emerge out of nowhere, how they can shock with their sudden violence, and how an animal is often changed afterwards as a result, either diminished and fearful, or aggressive and newly confrontational: broken.

I'm processing none of this right now, of course. I'm simply trying to keep them apart in the hope that the other Border's owner, a woman called Viv who is as long and thin as the cigarettes she smokes and who currently is responding to a text message on her Nokia, does something affirmative, and quickly. I half register the fact that there is blood on Missy's limb, and a flap of flesh, evidence of Mullet's first contact. I make a swiping motion with my hand that hits his head and sends him tumbling, but he's up again in an instant, jumping again, and snapping, and now he is actually hanging on to Missy's tail, swinging from side to side like the pendulum of a grandfather clock. This cannot be good, surely? Someone somewhere is shouting loudly. I think it might be me.

It is Lintang who brings things to a dramatic conclusion, this diminutive woman who has always been too shy and reluctant to engage in conversation but who now takes control of the situation with the definitive action that I clearly lack. She grabs Mullet by his own stubby tail, and yanks. The dog howls, and she flings him into the air where, for a moment, he flies like a frisbee. He lands with a thud, then jumps up but thinks twice about coming back for more, and instead just sits there, panting. Only now does Viv place her phone back into her pocket, and saunter over.

'All right,' she says, 'what's going on?'

She sees Missy breathing heavily in my arms, her nostrils flaring. A look of concern passes across Viv's face, and the blood drains from her cheeks.

It's barely eight o'clock in the morning. By rights, I shouldn't even be here. The morning is Elena's time, but she is busy today with work and so I'm deputising. A few minutes earlier, Mullet had wandered over, Viv assuring me that, 'Don't worry, he won't bite.'

I'd met Viv before, several times, but she never remembered. She was a woman with a public-facing expression of perpetual confusion, and who right now was consumed by the activity taking place on her phone. She was in her sixties, wore Wellington boots in all weathers, and had long grey hair tied into a ponytail that trailed down the length of her back. Her eyes were David Bowie's, one blue, the other brown. Mullet, her dog, quickly started growling at Missy, as was his habit. He had a reputation he worked hard to maintain, a perpetually garrulous enthusiasm that too often spilled over into something more, with teeth.

'He's just playing, that's all,' Viv would insist. 'Terriers do, don't they? I wish mine was as pretty as yours. What's his name?'

I told her.

'A girl? Sorry, thought he was a boy.'

Viv had the anxious mien of someone whose thoughts often assailed her unawares; even a smile came loaded with ambiguity. Her mouth was forever curved into a lowercase o, something that was ordinarily plugged by a cigarette but, for now at least, wasn't. Sometimes she used it to whistle to her dog. She was always friendly enough, and all too frequently apologetic for an animal she clearly had little control over.

'He's fine, honestly.'

She'd wandered off then, consumed by an incoming text message, leaving me to monitor a situation whose rules were at best ambiguous. At one point, Missy lost patience with Mullet and warned him to back off. This was when he launched himself at her. In the midst of the fight, I became aware of a very particular smell being emitted by one or other of them, or both. Fear? (It could have been me.) I only noticed the hammering of my heart after Lintang intervened, flinging Mullet away as she had, her accompanying karate cry bringing Viv back into the present world.

The fight lasted mere seconds. All that's left now is its post-match analysis, something for which I have neither the time nor the appetite. While Viv is rushing over to her dog, I feel the imperative to turn to Lintang to thank her, and to make sure she knows I'm grateful for her help.

She's busy stooping to retrieve the various leads of her own dogs, but when she's upright again I see a look of great pale shock on her face, as if her actions had surprised even herself. I notice that she's wearing a sweatshirt – it's late April by now, the days getting warmer, her Puffa jacket consigned to the winter wardrobe – and the sleeves have ridden up to expose her arms. I notice bruises on the skin of her left forearm, an imprint that looks like it might have been made by a tight grip, and by fingers that squeezed hard.

She sees me looking, then pulls quickly at the sleeves, and turns to leave. I thank her again, and she replies with a nod of the head. Then she's gone.

Viv strides over. 'He was only playing,' she tells me. 'Terriers, they get a bit frisky, right?'

I tell her that it's fine, and make to leave. But Viv has noticed the blood on Missy's flank, and she falls to her knees and attempts to brush the wound better, in case it counts as evidence. 'There,' she says, clearly agitated. 'All good. You're fine, Missy, aren't you?' Missy licks her on the nose.

Mullet slopes over, the dogs sniff one another, and then sit side by side with the inane insouciance of, well, of dogs. Viv accompanies me as we walk to the gate, and she is speaking quickly now, rapid-fire words falling over one another like tumbling dominoes. She tells me how the dog, which she says she got to combat loneliness, has turned out to be more trouble than he's worth.

'People complain about him, you know?' she says. 'Even when he's done nothing wrong, not really. Most people, you know, they don't react like you just did back there, calmly; no, they shout and scream, and threaten me. The police've been called! My nerves,' she says. 'It's not good for my nerves.'

Viv now slips her hand into the crook of my arm. 'You won't report me, will you? I'm already on a warning,

64

and Mullet didn't mean it, he didn't.' She looks at me beseechingly. 'I'm asking you nicely, as a friend. *Please?*'

I reassure her, and tell her that Missy's fine, mostly because I hope she is. Upon hearing her name spoken out loud, she looks up at me and wags her tail in anticipation. I give her a treat, and then offer one to Mullet too, because it seems rude not to.

But Viv isn't so easily pacified.

'Listen,' she says, pulling on my arm now as if to bring me to heel. 'How about I do you a reading to make up for it?' Her expression is earnest, pleading with me to say yes.

'A reading?'

'Yeah, yes. I'm a psychic, an animal psychic. I took a course, got a diploma and everything! But I've always been able to communicate with animals, since I was young. I give readings, people come to me to find out what their animals are thinking, and how they can understand them better. No,' she says, 'I know what you're thinking, I can't do it with him, with Mullet, never been able to – and I've tried, my God I've tried! An enigma, that one, a blank space. But I can do most other animals. I did it with horses as a child, and dogs, but not cats. Cats don't like their minds being read. But I've done loads of dogs, dozens, hundreds maybe. I've helped people track their dogs down when they've gone missing. They send out messages, the dogs, and I receive them. And I've also helped people just get to know their pets a little more, to improve their relationships, control bad behaviour, that kind of thing. I've been on TV for it. I have!'

'So let me read Missy for you, go on,' she implores. 'No charge!'

I look around, hoping for the diversion of a Pavlov or an Elizabeth, but it's not the right time for either of them, and all I see are unfamiliar people in Lycra, their dogs jogging faithfully alongside them. I make a show of looking at my watch, and explain that a reading really isn't necessary, that I'm late enough for work as it is.

Viv drops to her knees, and cradles Missy's head in the palms of her cupped hands. I expect my dog to withdraw, as she no doubt would with me, but she doesn't. Instead, she returns Viv's penetrating gaze. The intimacy makes me uncomfortable.

'Does she have an intolerance to wheat?' Viv asks. 'She's telling me that she has an intolerance to wheat.' She looks up at me. 'And she says that you might, too. Oh, she's very chatty, this one, lots to say! I know you'll think I'm mad – lots of people do – but I really do hear their voices. Anyone can, I think. You just need to know how to tune in, and listen.'

I check my watch again. Late is getting later.

Still from her kneeling position, the dog's chin resting patiently in her hands, Viv tells me that a horse once told her that its owner would one day fall in love with a woman with only four fingers on her left hand. A few years later, Viv says, 'He did! So how's that for proof? Because how else could I know a detail like that?'

This prompts an obvious question, of course: how could the horse?

'A snake,' she continues, 'once told me he was sad.'

She stands now, brushing mud from her knees. 'I know it sounds crazy, but one of the most difficult things about

this gift is simply speaking out loud what is being trans-
mitted by them to me. They say these things, and I can
only relay them. You can imagine what the snake's owner
told me when I told him that, that his pet might be
depressed! But he went out afterwards and bought a new
cage – vivarium, they're called – and he cheered right
up, so, you know?'

She picks Missy up now, and again Missy doesn't
resist. They look intensely at one another, and again I
look around me, scanning the edges of the park.

'She wants you to know,' Viv says, 'that things aren't
always as bad as they seem, and that you're doing okay,
you really are, despite, she says, despite *everything*. Does
that make sense to you?'

Seeing me blush, she adds, 'Sorry for the intimacy,
but that's what she's saying.'

They commune quietly again for a loaded moment,
and then Viv says: 'Eleven.'

'Eleven?'

'Yeah. Any significance? Like I say, I'm only the
messenger.'

I shrug.

'She's giving me a door with the number 11 on it. Is
that your door number? It isn't? Well, maybe you're
moving soon? You're not? Missy thinks you are, ha! She
says that she's okay with it.'

'But we're not moving,' I repeat, while at the same
time privately wondering: *are we?*

She tells me that in September a woman called
Caroline will come into my life with an intriguing work
offer. She reveals that Missy knows I once had an

67

ingrowing toenail. She says the dog prefers human food to its canine equivalent.

'And this is going to sound a little odd, but do you have a bad smell? In your car, I mean. Missy says she doesn't like it.'

I take a step back, and steady myself. A few months ago, our car, which was almost twenty years old and clearly ailing, began to issue noxious fumes. We ignored it, as we always do with car problems until the problem becomes unavoidably grave, which, duly, this one did. I explain now to Viv that we recently bought a new car, and that, as it happens, Missy does seem more comfortable in it. Viv nods her head in agreement. 'Yes, yes she is.'

There's more.

'Dieppe,' she says. 'Ever been? Missy is telling me Dieppe. France, isn't it? Maybe you'll go soon? She also says that you recently trained as a helicopter pilot. Have you?' Viv asks, sounding impressed. I look between her eyes, the blue one and the brown one, and the keen eagerness on her face, the encouraging smile. She laughs, entirely free of self-consciousness, and says again that she's only the messenger, and can only relay what she gets.

'It's funny,' she says, looking between her dog and mine. 'The things they come up with. You'd hardly believe it, would you?'

A month later, summer now, and the park is rife with gossip. Police were called to Viv's. A woman in a Barbour jacket, whose Border collie puppy wound up in a similar altercation with him, made a complaint. Mullet has been taken away. This woman, whom I'd occasionally seen training her dog on an extendable lead not simply to follow and to sit, but also to walk backwards and up on its hind legs, to beg and to play dead, had claimed that the fight had left her dog with PTSD. The vet had had to refer her to an animal psychologist. The woman had reported Mullet immediately, and then returned to the park the following day with a sheet of paper on a clipboard, a petition to have the dog removed, which she insisted people sign.

Few signed, because dog owners, I'm finding, are a loyal bunch, but Mullet was taken away regardless, in a small metal cage by a man wearing protective gear, Viv later telling Elizabeth that Mullet had failed to read the signs and instead greeted the dog handler with eagerness, as if convinced he was about to set off on an exciting new adventure. Which in one sense he was.

Viv vanishes from the park after that. More inexplicably, so too does the Barbour lady and her Border collie, despite their victory. The speculation over both their fates keeps everyone going quite comfortably until the next incident. In the dog park, there is always a next incident.

Over time, the story fades into folklore. In its multiple retellings, Mullet had in fact harmed countless dogs, and had maimed at least one, which, one concerned woman would later tell me, 'serves as a reminder that, you know, however domesticated, dogs are wild animals whose behaviour has to be monitored at all times.' She herself owned a Chihuahua which used any excuse to bare its pixie teeth.

I won't much think about the Barbour lady again after this, but Viv I will. I'll have particular cause to remember Viv.

Weeks go by, and one weekend Elena and I take a drive somewhere. We bring the dog. As usual, she jumps eagerly into the back seat, then steps forward onto the arm divide between the front seats, breathing her breath into our face and pointing her chin in the direction she'd like to go. But then, a moment later, she is quivering, and emitting a high whine, clearly distressed. We are confused. There is no old car bad smell, nothing newly untoward. On the outward journey she shivers throughout, and pants herself towards hyperventilation. This sets a precedent, and every time we take a car journey with her from now on, for at least the next two years, she shakes and pants, and whoever is unfortunate enough to sit next to her must bear her full weight which, when compounded by anxiety, feels as heavy as a Rottweiler's. We have no idea why she experiences this new fear, and so we draw only one conclusion about its likely provenance. It's been placed there, like a hex, by Viv – Viv, the sinister dog psychic who, like Mullet, is gone but, as Mullet must be for her, is never fully forgotten.

Six

We're on holiday when the news reaches us, by text: Billy has died. During hot summer months, the cat had liked to shelter under the wheels of parked cars. Normally, the sound of an engine starting was enough to rouse him from slumber and he'd move to a place of safety, but not this time.

The words don't digest at first. Not Billy, surely? I show the phone to Elena, who exhales sharply, and we share a look to convey our mutual disbelief. One of us shakes a head firmly, I can't remember who, but it communicates to the other the imperative not to tell the children, not yet at least. When we return home ten days later, the girls exit the taxi, discard their suitcases on the pavement, and run down the road calling for him, crying out his name, telling him they're back.

There are many moments in early parenthood that can break your heart. This is one of them.

'Where is he?' they say repeatedly, as the news we'd delayed telling cannot be delayed for very much longer.

The look for a dog begins in earnest soon after. We've an absence to fill. Propaganda merchants across social media upload footage of their pets at a rate of hundreds per second, and the girls assail us with video evidence frequently. Dogs being cute, doing cute things, doing alarming things; so very many dogs. The sound that comes from the girls is of heartstrings being plucked, and so a routine develops. Each afternoon after school, and most evenings after dinner, together we scour canine Tinder in search of our perfect match. We swipe endlessly left, with cursory unfeeling, all the older dogs, the angry dogs, the anxious dogs, and those with complicated pasts. We are first-time owners, and trying to eradicate the possibility of complication as best we can. But puppies are hard to find. Like gold, they have currency. The moment they surface online, available, they've gone.

One weekend, we drive to the big dogs' home in town, where that plaintive pluck of heartstrings swells towards the full Disney. There are rows and rows, in fact entire *floors*, of incarcerated animals, each searching – so the descriptive blurb attached to their gates advertises – for their forever homes. The Staffordshire terriers with their Joker smiles, the greyhounds whose boomerang bodies curl into themselves like timid commas, tails between legs, and the scruffy mutts comprised of a thousand motley ingredients. Together, they represent countless hidden stories of cruelty, abandonment, and misery. An interview with staff members confirms that we are not eligible for these sorts anyway. We are that problematical kind of adopter: novices, and with young children. We'd be best looking for young dogs, puppies, we're told, 'but we don't have any right now. They tend to go quick.'

We keep traipsing the floors anyway, and the time flies. Hours are lost in contemplation. At one point, I stop by an empty kennel, piqued by a sign that reads 'Alan'. Alan is a Norfolk terrier, almost two years old. A recent arrival, he had been admitted, so his information sheet reads, after his elderly owner had gone into hospital and could no longer look after him. While reading this, Alan emerges from the shadows. He walks into the middle of his cell, then sits very deliberately, and looks up at me.

I cannot explain what happens between myself and Alan in the few moments when we appraise one another between the bars of the gate that keeps him locked in, and me out. Where other dogs have either scowled at me or, more often, jumped about with the kind of excitement you would never get from cats, Alan instead keeps his own counsel. In his eyes, which are the colour of jade, I convince myself that I can see a cascade of emotion. There is an instinctive wariness, and there is pain too, and disappointment, but also hope and the distant intimations of trust. He is small and stocky, giddily handsome, with amazingly tidy paws and a thick coarse fur that bristles with autumnal hues. Never have I seen a more real-life manifestation of Paddington Bear.

At some point, my legs buckle.

From further down the corridor, I hear the girls calling out for Elena, telling her that they think I might be crying.

With a tilt of my chin, I motion towards Alan who, as they gather alongside me, turns now to look at them. The girls crouch down and hold out their hands in the hope of coaxing him over, to stroke his nose, to exchange scents, but diffident Alan remains where he is. He is weighing us up, and refuses to come to a decision in haste.

'Him!' the girls cry. '*Him!*'

Elena sidles up to me. 'Are you all right?' she says.

My voice is a whisper. '*Him.*'

It's a long walk back to reception, during which time we peer into all the other kennels out of politeness and respect. Although we'd all long ago decided on a puppy, Alan, who is fourteen in dog years, and the most pensive-seeming teenager I've ever encountered, is the one, the only one.

The drive back feels funereal. The home had explained that Alan required a family experienced in dogs. Yes, they concurred, he did seem friendly and gentle, but he could be snappy, too. He was greatly missing his owner, and would take time adapting to a new environment. He was not suitable for young children.

We've lost something we never had in the first place.

When I turn the radio on, the girls lean over and turn it back off again. They are insistent that the search continues the moment we get home.

And so we scroll through more and more pages. At first, we'd focused on dog websites, but now we have migrated to those sites that also sell cars and motorbikes, tents and tools, and offer cleaners and Spanish lessons. This does not feel like the optimum way to get a pet, but then the dogs' home is proving complicated, and each of us – even me – is growing impatient.

They put us on their waiting list, and instruct us to call every Wednesday afternoon in the hope that a new litter has arrived. If one has, they say, then we'll have to act quickly, as puppies don't hang around for long. The home closes each day at four o'clock, and school doesn't finish until half past three. The journey is almost ten miles. The logistics are against us, and so we look elsewhere. Canine Tinder throws up new litters all the time, and all are available, but none are close to home, and so our weekends now require early starts and motorway journeys. There is traffic. We have to stop at petrol stations for crisps and chocolate on the way, the calories fuelling our anticipation.

In deep country now, the motorway having given way to narrow meandering lanes, fewer shops, almost no people. We see tractors and unflashy 4x4s, hay bales and grazing cows. I see a horse tied to a pole, and the woman on the phone did mention the horse tied to a pole. It stares disconsolately at a wall in front of its face while scuffing its right shoe on the cobbles beneath, the sound of one hand clapping.

The woman emerges, the woman from the phone, and she leads us silently to a small barn piled high with haystacks and farm equipment I have no vocabulary for. In a penned-off corner lies a small brown dog beached on her side, teats distended, and around her four tiny puppies.

'Eight weeks almost,' the woman says.

She takes a step towards them but keeps going, to the back of one of the hay bales. From here she retrieves an even smaller dog, the runt of the litter. He'd been hiding. She holds it out to us in one hand.

'Here,' she says.

'A girl?' I ask for clarification.

'Male.'

'On the phone, you told us a girl.'

'These lot are the bitches, but they're sold now. He's lovely, this one.'

This is an all-new experience for us, and I've no idea of the etiquette. I'm wearing jeans and trainers, she's in overalls and industrial Wellington boots. I imagine that she looks at me, someone who drove in from the big city especially, the way Pavlov and I regarded the Barbour lady after she tried to get us to sign her petition against Mullet: with derision. A mischievous voice that arrives unbidden inside my head wants to tell her that we've come on holiday by mistake, and to ask if she's the farmer. I hold the dog, which feels light and warm in my hand, the very first puppy I've ever held, towards the girls, but he begins to squirm and I'm fearful of dropping him. I replace him carefully on to the floor of the barn, and we watch as he slinks immediately back behind the hay bale, blind and trembling.

'All right, then?' the woman says, impatient for the transaction to be completed. 'He's nervous, but he's fine. They're Jack Russell/King Charles spaniel cross. Really rare, really lovely dogs. I'd show you the dad, but the dad's a working dog, and he's out in the fields right now. But here's the mum, as you can see.' She points. 'See?'

His siblings dash around the pen, bright and alert. Only he cowers.

A sharp yip now fills the air, and the girls turn towards its likely source, another pen on the other side of the barn. The woman becomes animated.

'My beauties, these are, miniature Bichons Frise.'

They're the size of pom-poms. Eight of them congregate alongside another tired mother. 'Six weeks old,' she tells us, 'but they're expensive, these ones. Need to sell the others first. So?'

Her impatience returns.

'Get him into the car and back to yours, and he'll be fine,' she says.

'Cash only,' she says.

Missy is one of ten, which probably accounts for why the mother looks so very exhausted, lying flat out in another rural outhouse, this one absent of hay but filled instead with the detritus of a professional painter and decorator. Outside in the driveway is a car on bricks. I fight the impulse to deduce that this is another bad sign, because at this rate we'll never secure a dog, and the girls might never forgive me. The seller is a broad woman in faded dungarees who encourages me to make my choice. They all look the same, all running madly around the room in pursuit of something that plainly isn't there. I pick one at random, and she daubs a glob of white paint on its ear, takes a down payment, and tells me to come back tomorrow.

'Not today?' I ask. The drive had taken two hours.

'Tomorrow.'

Part of wanting to become a dog owner now is simply to have *all this* in the past.

The following day, on the way home, an as-yet-unnamed Missy sits on my lap, the girls on either side of me. Elena drives. I feel an astonishment that the dog we've just paid good money for is actually ours, a commitment that will probably last many years. I'll be objectively old when she dies. We take turns in stroking her gently. She has just been wrenched from her birth mother forever, but the seller had told us not to worry. 'It's natural,' she said. The dog is trembling, or perhaps I am? The smell that comes off her is extraordinary. Twice, she vomits into my crotch.

Her left ear will bear traces of the white paint for many weeks.

The impractical practicalities of owning a dog had lined up like dominoes but, as with dominoes, proved easy to topple. The initial impetus may have been sparked by the girls behaving like children, craving a dog much as they'd once craved a new toy, but I think we ultimately agreed to one for our benefit, too. After several difficult years, I craved distraction.

When I read the scientific research that explains how the body renews its cells every seven years, the associated assumption being that every seven years we are somebody new entirely, I latch onto it with a desperation common to anyone with ongoing health issues. I've already endured five years of fundamental physical change brought on by that initial bout of ill-health that, like Miss Havisham's dolour, never quite lifted, and so who's to say that the next few years might not see me renewed into someone else? Those cells could rejuvenate, and the brain, which I keep reading is plastic, figuratively speaking, might rewire itself differently. The brain does not remould out of inertia, or passivity. And so this poor dog represents something more than she might be able to handle, but surely not more than she can bear: a middle-aged man's hope.

It is harder to name her than we expected. We discount dozens, possibly hundreds, scrolling through dog names online until they all blend into a thousand Milos and Lunas. For the first forty-eight hours she is Lola, which is fine by me because I like The Kinks, but then several other dogs in the park are called Lola, and so she reverts, at least for a short while, to 'the dog', which, if nothing else, suits her. It is only after I show the girls the video to Missy Elliott's 'Get Ur Freak On' that, finally, we agree on something and finally christen her accordingly, partly in deference to America's first woman of hip hop, partly pressed into it by the insurance company which

79

needs a name quickly if they are going to accept our monthly dividends.

At eight weeks, she fits into my cupped hands. Like a newborn, her main preoccupation is to sleep. She grows, and each morning she seems a little longer, taller, broader. Gradually, she changes colour too, from a rich black to a russety brown. Her belly remains as pink as a pig, as soft as velvet. At first, she cries all night long, the saddest of songs. We'd been warned of this. 'Don't worry,' the seller had said, 'it just means that she's missing her mum and her siblings. She'll get over it.'

The girls had cried right along with her at the start, insurmountable remorse at having stolen her from her kin, which ultimately proved surmountable after all. Elena took to sleeping with her in the kitchen for the first few nights, as Missy upon waking would be frantic for company, and craving bodily contact. She duly pees and shits all over the floor, and in doing so makes a mockery of the seller's suggestion that she'd prove quick to toilet train. She doesn't. Over the next six months, Missy will pee and shit whenever the urge asserts itself, very often upstairs in my office, my carpeted office, while gazing lovingly at me from across the other side of the room. The very moment this happens, of course, I jump up and cry out in annoyance, rushing to reposition the sheets of newspaper scattered across the floor underneath her, newspaper she always manages to miss, but by then it's too late: another puddle to sink into the fabric and to stain a dull yellow, so many of these stains overlapping one another like a Venn diagram of pet-ownership frustration.

The man who comes to replace our carpets many

months later at eye-watering expense, someone who drives a Mercedes and plays golf at the weekends, tells me that *his* dog lives in a kennel out in the garden.

'Boundaries,' he says.

She has the run of the house very quickly. Whatever she wants, she gets. We will be strict with our *next* dog, we decide. I peer down at her frequently, all the time in fact, as if keen to double-check that her presence is real, this thing that is very much *not* a cat. When we had children, I remember there being a slow process of acclimatisation, of getting to know these two small people we now had to look after and protect, forever. The love I felt for them was tempered undeniably by terror: I had no idea what to do with them, nor how to look after them, not properly, as parents must. It took weeks, *months*, before I started to feel in any way approaching a functioning father. But the connection to Missy feels quicker – more natural, almost. I *know* how to look after animals, they are easier than humans, more robust, fewer demands. The fact that her presence will now alter my life is something I embrace. All I have to do is gaze at her – those handsome limbs, the twitching nose and panting tongue, the adoring eyes – and stupidly I melt. I know nothing of science, but I decide it must be doing wonders for my serotonin levels.

She spends most of the day on my lap, unmoving, and perfectly content – not purring, true, but the warmth's nice. I learn to ignore the demands of my bladder. On more than one occasion, a mid-morning knock at the door that might well be the postman bringing me important mail is ignored entirely. I don't want to disturb her. And when I *do* disturb her, she follows wherever I go. One time, when I must absolutely get to the toilet quickly, she comes with me, watching while I position my trousers around my ankles and sit. A moment later, she clambers into my puddled boxer shorts and curls up in the gusset, glancing up at me just to check that I'm still there, and then she falls once more into her perpetual slumber.

This marsupial closeness is more intimacy than I'd bargained for.

Seven

Pavlov scowls, to reveal a set of many-years-undentisted teeth.

I'd been telling him about dog mystic Viv, now vanished, and how she compensated for the recent attack by Mullet by offering to read Missy's mind. The scowl collapses his eyebrows into a V shape with such a strong pull of gravity that his frown falls down into his eyes.

'And you *let* her?'

I wasn't given much choice, I tell him, and add that, 'besides, my dog was oddly compliant.'

'*No*,' he says. 'You should not indulge this woman.'

When I ask why, he shakes his head.

'I don't like it. She cannot mind-read, for start, is

impossible. But also, who wants to know what is going on in their dog's head? My dog's thoughts,' he says, 'is something I want to guess for myself – to, to intuit. You know? This is why we have animals, to navigate the distance between us, to find common ground. We communicate *despite* language barrier, and we do not need such people,' he means Viv, 'to build us these bridges. I do not want her to come along and facilitate this for me, or to pretend she does.

'Communicating with your animal,' he continues, 'and trying to understand one another, this is why man and animal is so close, yes? This is why is magic, to have pet. I speak to Dog every day, and he speaks to me, and we understand each other better than I understand anyone else in whole world. So I don't need this, this . . . *woman*, to tell me anything about that.'

It's a warm day verging on hot, which means that Pavlov has left the flying jacket at home. He wears his regulation black T-shirt, which is stretched across his torso like clingfilm. I can see what he had for breakfast on it, certain of the stains indicative of egg. I haven't seen him for almost a week now, work demands and a rebounding bout of fatigue having left me sofa-bound for days, and so Pavlov feels he has much ground to make up. He tells me that Elizabeth has been poorly with a virus. Her elder daughter has come from the coast to look after her – the other lives in Australia, and Zooms every other day – and she walks Betty at different, and for shorter, times. Their paths don't cross. An extended bout of boredom, then, has turned him verbose.

He tells me about his latest run-in with the doctor,

who refuses to chase the pending hospital appointment despite the fact of his ongoing pain. He never seems to get any further along in the waiting list, and so in the meantime he's self-medicating more.

'I have to drink, it helps. Some vodka each night, but no hangover in the morning, at least. Small consolation, huh? You know me, I don't like to complain,' he adds, '*but.*'

To offset all the pain, memory lane. As we walk, he tells me about his youth, which resides for him, cinematically, in the rearview mirror, and he tells me again of all the people he hung out with during his time in New York – artists, creatives, mafiosi.

'After club we go to Meatpacking District for drugs and deals and breakfast bagels. Such times,' he sighs.

He namedrops with a gleeful abandon, and, later, a professional instinct prompts me to Google both for more information *and* corroboration. I learn that his attention to detail does seem suspiciously like the truth, and I am now required to consider him a man of hidden depths, someone whose tall tales might actually be of average height, after all. The fact that he once led such a heady life makes me happy for him; that it is now comprehensively over makes it easy to empathise.

Many of his conversational strands take him back to the mother country, and the impact it had on him. He is no longer an admirer of Russia, he says. (Some years later, he will wear with pride a Ukrainian badge, which he ordered off the internet from China.) He talks again about his months in hospital recovering from the road traffic accident, and also from those vague subsequent complications, whose consequences would prove lifelong.

'Russia back then was like dark ages,' he says, claiming that if the nurses were merciless, then the doctors were even worse.

When eventually he was discharged, his left leg had withered, and would never regain full muscle definition. The hair on his head no longer grew fully across his scalp, which was now interrupted by twenty-six stitches. For the remainder of his teen years, he developed a comb-over, but by early adulthood had committed to shaving his head, which he hid with a hat. (The ponytail would not arrive until midlife.) It was during his early twenties, in America, where he learned to use his afflictions to his benefit. He tells me that he was popular with women who read the novels of J. G. Ballard and watched the films of David Cronenberg. He used their fascination with his scars to his advantage. 'You work with what you've got, yes?'

Though only a decade separates us, he likes to talk to me about ageing, convinced he's providing me with the kind of valuable information that stretches towards wisdom. 'To prepare you,' he says, the father I never knew. His need to vent becomes increasingly evident, and to allow it feels almost like a charitable act.

'This age,' he says. 'This is difficult age. Is like we have no future, like all the best things already happen to us. *But!* We must be practical about future, we must prepare. We must live still.'

He worries over the fate of Dog should anything happen to him, and at the same time clings to the animal the way a drowning man would a buoy. The bulk of the pleasure he derives from life now comes mostly from a three-legged Staffordshire terrier.

'You have noticed, yes,' he says, 'that connection – with other people, I mean – it gets harder for us the older we get?'

He laments lost friendships, lost loves, and a swollen sense of aloneness, but pushes back against even the prospect of pity by insisting that, in fact, he welcomes it, calling it a fact of life, the inevitable collective fate of us all. The maintenance of friendship, he tells me, requires effort, and after a certain age each of us is too old for effort.

He looks at me for corroboration. 'I am right, yes?'

I look back at him, my strange new friend, and see a mixture of emotions work away at his features. He looks eager, and craves agreement; he seems crestfallen, and hopes to conceal it. I know enough now to realise that when he begins talking like this, it can be difficult to stop him. A half-hour dog walk can stretch to four times as long. We've already completed four laps of the park now. Even if I weren't prone to tiredness, I'd be exhausted. He scans the place for Dog, sees him rooting around one of the bins, and calls him over.

'One more lap, yes?' he encourages.

He tells me that women are different: better, kinder, and imbued with an empathy that men lack. He admires, he says, how women continue to reinvent themselves throughout life, creating new friendships and nurturing new networks.

'But not us. I mean, look at all the other men we see around here every day, walking their dogs. Are they with partners, or with their friends, or are they alone, like us?'

The park is busy right now. He points to Keith, surely

sweating in his white denim, alone with his thoughts, his Alsatian and cockatoo, and to Sid and Rocky, the latter too hot to bother with the basketball today. Earlier, I'd seen Wilson on his habitual powerwalk while the family dog trotted only semi-faithfully behind him. There is the man who spends most of every afternoon here, taking over one of the benches with his multiple carrier bags, sitting in between them staring intently into his iPad while his scruffy mutt sleeps beside him. And there is another regular, a tall individual crouched in an impressive display of balance while smoking a cigarette and dictating long passages into his phone. He is always talking into his phone while his Dobermann tests the parameters of his peripheral vision. I heard some of the dictation once. 'I don't know what your problem is full stop new line,' he spoke. 'Why can't you just speak to me like a normal person question mark exclamation mark.'

'All of them,' Pavlov says, 'all of *us*: alone. Coincidence? Accident? No!'

He takes me by surprise now when he starts to croon, a vaguely familiar song from decades past about having no further need for social networks, and how friendship only causes pain.

'Very poetic,' I say.

'Not me, Paul Simon. But is true, no? You and me,' he says, 'we would not be friends outside this park. And, Nick, I wouldn't want to see you anywhere else but here. Please, take no offence!' He grins. 'Is enough here. Is relaxed and easy, undemanding. We just talk here, and it does us good, passes the time. It is good,' he says, tapping the side of his head, 'for the mental health. Mint?'

I look over to him, and see he's offering me a Polo, not from the packet but rather loose. Two sit in the palm of his hand alongside other things retrieved from his pocket: a few coins, his house key, a tiny screwdriver, lint. I take one.

Sid and Rocky come over, saliva dangling from the dog's jawline like cheap jewellery as he huffs heavily, their presence abruptly consigning our conversation to history, or at least to be resumed another time. There is an established atmosphere between these two men, a not entirely comfortable one, and one I wouldn't know how to navigate. Sid and Pavlov rarely exchange much more than a cursory greeting unless forced into it, and I wonder whether they are simply *too* alike to ever fully get along, thereby proving Pavlov's thesis on the Difficulty of Men.

The small talk he claims to loathe now begins in earnest. He greets Sid with a nod of the head, an audible 'hello' and 'nice day', and then we each look up in the general direction of the sun as if to take in its heat. Rocky climbs aboard the scooter and settles between Sid's feet, desperate for any shade that might be available. My phone vibrates again.

'I should really go,' I say.

The unmistakable shrill barking of three excitable Pomeranians suddenly rends the air, and the three of us look over to see Lintang arrive. She's wearing a hoodie despite the heat, which frames her face into a picture-frame oval and, if anything, draws even more attention to it. Her lip is split, and swollen. There is bruising around her right eye, a mark livid enough to seem freshly imprinted. When she sees us, she turns abruptly away.

89

But too late, Pavlov's seen her. 'What in hell?'

He marches over, prompting me and Sid to follow. I wish that Elizabeth were here, a gentler presence to dilute his bluster.

His voice booms. 'Hey! What happen? What happen to you?'

We are upon her now, effectively cornering her to the edge of the park. Her dogs gaze up with interest. Lintang still cannot maintain eye contact, and instead merely glances fleetingly at Pavlov. She shakes her head, and attempts a smile that fades on formation. Tears pool in her eyes.

'I fell,' she says. 'It's nothing, I'm fine.'

She starts to walk purposefully away, dragging the dogs behind her. 'Bye bye,' she says.

Pavlov shakes his head, and says, 'No, *no*.' He calls out to her again, and begins to follow, encouraging us to do likewise. Abruptly, into the calm of this balmy afternoon previously dominated by male lecture, comes drama. I cannot help but see the scene from an objective vantage point, three men in pursuit of a small woman bearing evidence of a recent physical attack. The optics aren't good.

Eight

During the first few weeks of ownership, the girls rise early with an anticipation redolent of Christmas morning. They want to go downstairs to see her, but are timid unless accompanied by one of us. At first, the dog sleeps in the kitchen, in a crate, as recommended by the internet. But the crate is ostensibly a cage, and even with its door open it strikes for us the wrong note, and so we collapse it, and put it under the sofa where it's forgotten, left to collect dust. She sleeps instead on an overstuffed cushion that she appears to like. She wakes at dawn.

The girls' body clocks adjust accordingly, and they rouse us and rush downstairs. The alarm clock shows barely 6 a.m. Missy is teething, which means that she has begun to bite. She grazes like a cow, but on fingers and thumbs, the flesh of an exposed wrist, all ten toes. She bites through socks, often she draws blood. The girls are captivated by her but also wary of the wild animal in our midst. The gerbils were nothing like this. When the dog wants to play, it is my arm they proffer.

For weeks she remains the most unknowable thing, full of intent but also an innate clumsiness. She appears to feel no pain, and is curious about all things. Watching her navigate her new home becomes a spectator sport. The toilet training remains a disaster. There is celebration when she manages for the first time to climb the stairs without tumbling backwards into our waiting arms, but this increased mobility means that she can now defecate anywhere she pleases. She uses shoelaces as dental floss, is fascinated by the sound of the extractor fan, the TV, and the postman's knock. And although she is never quite funny enough for TikTok, I find myself recording her endlessly, filling up valuable storage space on my phone with videos that no one needs to see.

Soon, she requires socialising. Until inoculations are given, she has to be carried wherever she goes. Like a historical royal, her feet don't touch the ground. Each afternoon, I cradle her small but squirming form in my arms and take her with me to the school gates to collect the girls. We are surrounded by crowds who tend collectively towards the excitable, and I feel like the manager of a pop star trying to protect my charge from paparazzi. I'm Brian Epstein to her Paul McCartney; she is arrestingly cute. I have by this stage in my life become used to moving through the world invisibly, the focus of precisely nobody. But now, with the dog, that changes. The simple process of walking down the road causes strangers to look, to catch their breath and clamp a hand to their chest, to sigh audibly, and to come up to me. 'Can I stroke him?' is a plea I hear a dozen times a day. The parallels with parenthood are evident. Everyone has an opinion on how to raise her, and they feel it their business to tell me. I'm told what to feed her, and also what not. In a busy street market one Saturday afternoon, a middle-aged woman approaches, telling me that she simply must pick up my dog and cradle her.

'I had a Border too,' she says. 'Make sure to never let her get to fat, okay? These are hunting dogs, they go down rabbit holes. It's in their nature. But the holes are small, you understand?'

I'm standing in front of this woman in awkward listening pose, the lead now hanging redundant by my side because my dog is in her arms, and she is telling me a story from childhood, how her father lost his Border for days. Days! 'I mean, can you imagine? This was in the countryside, a farm, and we spent day and night searching for him, going out of our minds.'

Elena and the girls, who'd been browsing in a shop, come out to join me. They do not look surprised by the woman's attentions; all of us have quickly become used to it.

'I'm just telling your dad,' she says to the girls, 'not to let the dog get fat, okay? *Okay?* So yes,' she says, picking up the earlier thread, 'we looked for him every-where. Where did we find him?' I shrug my shoulders, no earthly idea. 'Just out of a rabbit hole, blackened with dirt, all giddy in the daylight. He must have got stuck, and so he did the only thing he could do: wait. He'd licked the ground around him for the moisture, but he was getting increasingly hungry, of course, and then starving. Three days and nights! He lost weight, got skinnier, enough to eventually wriggle free.'

They'd previously been feeding him on scraps, she says. 'He got stocky round the middle. Never let a Border get stocky round the middle. You want to maintain the S shape of the stomach.' She puts the dog down now, and traces Missy's S shape. Oddly, I feel a flare of pride. This woman is praising my dog's figure. 'Keep her like this, okay? And if you ever do lose her, look for the rabbit holes!'

Another day, another woman comes up to me in the street, and scoops Missy up without forewarning, then drapes her across her right shoulder.

'See? She balances!' she says joyfully.

The dog gets her inoculations, and begins to walk. Her perfect paws grow hardened and scratched, newly rough to the touch. Her coat continues to change from black to brown. She learns to tilt her head like the dogs on the television, knowing full well the response it elicits. People repeatedly tell us she's unusually good-looking for a Border, a breed that can sometimes tend towards the gremlin-like, and that initial pride I felt swells to epic proportions, as if *I* am personally responsible. One warm Sunday afternoon, I take the dog and the girls to a nearby common where we come across a neighbourhood dog show. Somebody gives me a flyer. BEST IN SHOW COMPETITION, 3 P.M. ALL WELCOME. I object to beauty pageants on principle, I think, but the girls insist, and so by mid-afternoon I find myself parading my new dog alongside fifteen others of various breeds, mixes and ages. Ours is by far the prettiest, of this I have never felt more sure.

When she doesn't make any of the three placings, not gold, silver or bronze, I am furious, blindsided with rage. I want to remonstrate with the judges. The girls pull me away. I brood over the insult for days.

People continue to flock to her wherever we go. Far more sociable than I have ever been, the dog wants to meet *everyone*, and to be the recipient of their cooing attention. For the first eighteen months of her life, she loves nothing more than other dogs. She likes to sink her teeth into the scruff of their necks – something I'm told is an overture of friendliness, though I have my doubts – which prompts both of them to tear off around the park at speed, connected like Siamese twins. The park etiquette that Pavlov likes to speak about soon reveals itself, and I begin to identify two very different sets of people: the newcomers, like me; and the old hands. The former are nervous, still unsure of their animals and uncomfortable with the attentions of other, larger ones; the latter tend to preach, like priests, on the importance of socialisation, and the need for us to simply step back and let them get on with it. A few bites here and there, so Pavlov says, is nothing to get alarmed by. The dogs don't harbour resentment. 'Leave them be!' he urges. Many people here tend to give the old hands like Pavlov, and his hobbling mutt, as wide a berth as they possibly can.

One afternoon Pavlov says: 'Okay, so do you want to

understand just how anxious the average human being is? Watch them when they get dog. A dog is only as nervous as his owner. So many dogs here, they are crazy. And that's because their people are crazy. They should calm down, you know. Dogs will be dogs.'

Helplessly self-conscious around Pavlov, I methodically train myself not to be a nervous owner, and to give the dog the freedom she needs and craves. If she wants to run, let her run. She'll come back. Every park has its share of horror stories, however, of those that don't, instead bolting madly out of their green spaces and into the traffic with tragic consequences. I am regularly told, with a curious relish, tales of dogs who find gaps in the railings and then meet a car head-on. Elizabeth once told me of having to witness a dog die from such a collision, and then having to cope with the owner afterwards, whose catastrophic reaction required her to call an ambulance for him.

I sign up for dog-training classes. The classes are run by a brusque woman who says that we will meet at a particular park at eight o'clock every Saturday morning 'come rain or shine', but who in the event fails to turn up whenever it's either too cold or too wet. 'Never let your dog onto the furniture,' she instructs. 'Never let them upstairs. Never feed them from the table. Do not be afraid to scold.' She says that dogs must be aware of the familial hierarchy, they must know who's boss. 'Do not tolerate their separation anxieties. When they howl, hit them once across the prow of the nose with a rolled-up newspaper, light but firm. They'll soon stop. Don't indulge them. They're dogs, not humans.'

I soon stop going to dog-training classes.

The world around us shrinks. I find that we're barred entry from all sorts of places that were once open to us: cafes, restaurants. Public transport becomes problematical – other passengers; all the opening and closing of doors; so many shuffling and careless feet. When we do find accommodating places to frequent, the dog refuses to sit, to lie or stay still, but instead becomes ravenously fascinated by the new terrain with its heady brew of provocative smells. She pulls constantly at her lead, straining towards other tables to charm and irritate, where she whimpers for scraps, and is desperate to follow the waiting staff to wherever it is they disappear behind those intriguingly heavy doors. When one of us leaves the table, however briefly – to go to the toilet, say – she breaks out into a tortured howl that sounds like Kate Bush at her most haunted. Dogs do not like the pack to be separated. This is cute and sweet, but also not. We now possess the ability to change the atmosphere of every place we enter, and to be the recipient of public censure and complaint.

It becomes difficult visiting certain friends. Some are unsure of dogs, or else not particularly fond. Is she toilet trained, they want to know, and we assure them that she is, mostly. Whenever she *is* permitted access to new homes, I have to watch her like a hawk for the entirety of our visit, unable to fully relax, poised to swoop the moment she either squats or looks like she might be readying herself to squat, at which point I whisk her up into the air leaving her wondering what on earth is happening. And all the while our hosts watch on, if not fully unamused then at least uncertain, put out. There are accidents, and profuse apologies. We buy flowers and bottles of wine as peace offerings. Some friends learn to be understanding; some don't invite us back.

Hers is a breed that doesn't moult, so the fact that her fur is *everywhere* remains a mystery. It's on our clothes, the sofa, in the butter and the jam. Her smell, too, which has the pungency of rolling tobacco and days' old biscuits, lingers in the air, on the carpets, and deep within the duvets. It's a smell never fully masked by any cleaning agent.

Over time, she assigns roles to each of us, to which we find ourselves dutifully sticking, as if spellbound. Elena she designates the sensible one, the leader of the pack. It was Elena who'd slept alongside her on those first early mornings when she was still acclimatising to her new home, and Elena who takes her for her walk first thing each morning. The girls she likes and even loves, but their relationship is on more even terms; they are equals. I am second-in-command, the joker in the pack. It's me she plays with because she knows that I will play back, often irrespective of other commitments. It's me who, energy levels permitting, runs with her in the park, and throws balls, and me who plays tug-of-war with her at home with anything to hand. I routinely find myself interrupting my lunch half-hour to run up and down the stairs and into various rooms, hiding from her while she seeks, a game she always initiates at the stroke of midday. On occasion, I've been late in responding to work emails because I'm stuck cowering in the cupboard under the stairs while she, with increasing desperation, tries to find me, yelping like a seal. Is this appropriate adult behaviour? Perhaps not, but it's such fun. If I had a tail, I'd be wagging it too. And it's me she turns to every afternoon to tell me it's time for another walk, always entirely unconcerned with my state of mind and body, whether it's raining or not. She knows only that her needs override most things and so, she urges, stop wasting time, and let's just *go*.

And, I find, I always do.

Despite the overwhelming suggestion that none of us really knows what we are doing here, she survives, lives, and somehow grows into a curiously well-behaved addition to the family. We've been lucky. There is no separation anxiety. She does not chew shoes or the wainscoting, the wifi cables remain unmolested, and she is at last fully toilet trained. In parks, she mostly comes back when called, and isn't afraid of traffic noises or motorbikes backfiring, as other dogs here are. She won't fear fireworks until she reaches the age of seven when, suddenly, she will. She doesn't bite the postman, does not roll in fox shit, and has yet to run away. When she vomits, which is rarely, she does not lap it back up again as I've heard dogs do but rather waits for me to deal with it. She becomes perfectly habituated to her surroundings, and behaves appropriately for a suburban dweller. We are never entirely sure what it is we have done right, but then that doesn't really matter. We've happened upon that most prized possession: a good dog.

She comes to dictate the tempo of our lives like a conductor does an orchestra. Everything operates to the beat of her drum. In the early days, when I was still following internet instructions, we'd forbidden her to sleep on beds, and she'd compliantly obeyed. But after renovations in the house that created two children's bedrooms where previously there had been just one, she decides that this ushers in for her a new dawn, with new rules. Now she sleeps on whichever bed takes her fancy. At first, we order her off, but not for long. It's just that she looks so terribly comfortable basking in that lozenge of sunshine on the clean white duvet. Instead of reprimanding her, I end up taking photographs of this dazzling beauty, and leaving her be. She personifies peace in the world.

It's in this way that she teaches us to fit *our* lives around *her*. She punches above her weight. Within a few short but incident-packed months, her ascendancy is complete, the household's hierarchy set in stone. The dog's the boss.

Nine

Agatha is the park's matriarch, its reliable focal point. Whenever she's here, there's an almost gravitational pull towards her, and not simply because my dog leads me with predictable impatience. She is a striking woman. Like Prince, her favourite pop star, she has a fondness for the colour purple that borders on obsession. Since his passing, it's the only colour she wears. She has purple hair and purple eye shadow, and her clothes are a combination of its many and varied hues: mauve, thistle, orchid, grape. She is not on Farrow & Ball's advisory board, but should be. She had bought herself some white trainers, but painted them herself in colours she described to me as lavender and *boysenberry*, a word I had to later Google.

She's in her mid-fifties, third-generation Caribbean, and is active on dating sites, building up by stealth a collection of catastrophic first dates that she will happily milk for their humour quotient in front of me but which, I sense, leave her feeling increasingly alone and adrift.

'Tears of a clown,' is what Pavlov says of her, unflatteringly. If he never seems, to me at least, entirely comfortable around her, then it's likely due to her strong personality, one that is more dominant, and ultimately more palatable, than his. She won't suffer his stories willingly, and pursues a habit of interrupting with some of her own the moment she observes him building up a head of steam. This is humanity in microcosm: in every community there are those who struggle in the role of support act, where others are born to shine. In the event of war, it will be Agatha who leads everyone down into the underground bunker, not Pavlov.

She's funny and flirtatious, heavyset yet disarmingly light on her feet – she loves to dance – and clearly thrives in her role as an art teacher at a local primary school, where I imagine the children must adore her. For someone of such eccentric individuality, I was surprised when she told me that her dog, a handsome French bulldog, was named Coco. Forty-five per cent of all dogs today are called Coco. *Her* Coco is an animal that is much beloved, and who behaves accordingly, as if convinced he is entirely deserving of the worship. His plump figure bears testament to the fact that she feeds him well, lean beef and broccoli stems, chicken breasts and green beans, pork medallions and alfalfa sprouts. Like a new mother, Agatha will interrupt any conversation she is in the midst of if Coco suddenly requires her attention. Though he can walk perfectly well, she likes to stroll through the park with him tucked under her arm like an expensive clutch bag. She refers to him as, 'My beautiful little man.'

Agatha had been watching our exchange with Lintang today, her interest further alerted when the three of us – me, Pavlov, Sid – had begun following and calling out to her. That lightness on her feet means that, Coco clamped securely under her arm, she reaches us quickly. She demands to know what's happening, and obligingly each of us comes to a standstill, Sid removing his hand from his mobility scooter's accelerator altogether. Pavlov fills her in, like a child reporting to the headmaster.

'We need to find out if she's all right,' Sid says, adding, 'but it might be better if *you* go to her.' Beside me, Pavlov bristles at the demotion to second billing.

'Darling! Hey, love?' Agatha runs on ahead, Coco's rear end staring back at me with its blind eye, his body still tucked within the crook of her arm. '*Hey!*'

Lintang stops, but reluctantly, and I watch from a distance as Agatha fires searching questions at her. She gathers up the smaller woman into a crushing embrace (specifically crushing Coco), leaving Lintang's arms to hang loosely by her side. Slowly, like the rubberneckers we are, we approach.

'Anything we can do to help?' Sid wonders aloud.

We form an imperfect circle around her. She looks helpless, and discomfited by our presence.

'I must go,' Lintang says imploringly, as if we're holding her against her will. '*Please?*' she says.

Agatha is not easily dissuaded. In the kind of gentle

tones she no doubt employs in the classroom, she asks again what happened. Lintang repeats her claim. 'I fell,' she says. 'But it's okay.'

What we know of her at this point remains limited. We know that the dogs aren't hers, and that she is required to walk them as part of her job. We know that her English is perfect, but that her demeanour is less certain of itself. She seems almost childlike in her timidity, but clearly isn't. When, a few weeks back, she stepped in to help me after the dog attack, I saw perhaps a glimpse of her true self, someone with a strong moral code, and also bravery. I've remained grateful to her ever since, and on nodding terms whenever we see one another. But she's always in a hurry and, unlike certain people here, I don't think it a requirement to befriend *everyone*, especially those in whom I register a certain reluctance. The Pomeranians are a daily duty for her, and she's impatient to get back.

But now she needs help. Part of me is still concerned by the optics, all of us bullishly coming to the aid of someone clearly in peril but who might not fully welcome it, or know quite what to do with it. But Agatha takes enviable control. She says that she is going to walk back with Lintang and, she adds, speaking directly to her, 'I won't take no for an answer!' She beams a smile at her, drapes a heavy arm around her, and off they go.

'If there's anything we can do, love, just let us know,' says Sid, and she nods while gathering her dogs together, and allowing Agatha, as if she had any other choice, to lead her away. I wait for eye contact from the school-teacher, a nod of tacit understanding between us, but

she's focused entirely on her pupil now, and I – all of us
– have been dismissed.

After they've left, we shuffle around in an awkward
silence into which, ultimately, we can only introduce
idle speculation, wonder, and gossip. It passes the time.
Benji ambles by, reliably stoned.

'What'd I miss?' he asks.

We do another couple of laps until, one by one, each
of us complains about the heat, and peels away.

After we've dispersed, my curiosity, which is rarely
dormant, leads me the long way home, along Spring
Grove, where Lintang lives and works. It is by some
distance the most expensive street in the neighbourhood.
It's also the strangest, designed erratically and almost
confoundingly, with every kind of domicile stacked up
alongside one another so that they sit – terraced, semi-
detached, fully detached – like a mouth crowded with
uneven or broken teeth. There's a small block of flats
alongside a row of two-up two-downs, some set back
from the road, others hugging the kerb. Several are in
visible disrepair, with clouded-over windows, crumbling
windowsills and long-ignored gardens. I imagine that
these are the homes of the street's oldest residents, those
that haven't taken advantage of gentrification and escal-
ating house prices. Outside one of them sits a years-dead
three-decade-old Saab estate upon which moss has begun
to grow, while weeds sprouting up from somewhere have
tied its useless door handles into leafy green knots.

The grander residences congregate towards the end

of the road. There are four in total, two on either side, each sitting behind its own high private wall, and boasting iron entry gates. I wonder what such houses are doing in a road like this, how they were transplanted here in the first place, or else how they survived being bisected into flats. Each of them dominates their immediate surroundings with an arrogant pride, throwing out shadows upon all those who pass beneath them.

Lintang's house is at the end, on the corner, by far the biggest. Beyond its gate are five steps that lead up to a grand front door, painted black, number 11. On either side of it are huge windows which, when not reflecting the sun, give glimpses of life within: a piano in one, a chandelier in the other; one tall bookcase heavy with books. The house rises to four floors, including basement and loft. More chimney stacks litter its roof than seem strictly necessary. It looks both handsome and ominous, the perfect location in which to set a psychological thriller. I imagine spiral staircases, locked rooms, floorboards that creek underfoot.

I try not to stare as I pass, but it's hard not to, knowing that somewhere within is Lintang, and knowing, too, that whatever happened to her that resulted in the bruising, happened in *there*.

The following day, Agatha offers an update. Though a compassionate person, she is not necessarily the soul of discretion. She tells us that Lintang is thirty-nine years old, and was sent here from Indonesia four months ago to become a live-in cleaner for a diplomat, though she has since had cause to believe that the man of the house isn't a diplomat at all but rather a more vague government underling clinging to an outpost far from home. He is not a nice employer, disinclined to both empathy and kindness.

She has been a domestic cleaner for many years. With no available work at home, she and many other young women, men too, were forced to look overseas. Cleaners were always required right across the developed world, and if you were fluent, and prepared to travel, there would always be jobs somewhere. Lintang was both. She had worked in Saudi Arabia and Hong Kong, and had returned to Jakarta after her marriage had ended, her now ex-husband having abandoned their two teenage daughters to Lintang's parents. But her parents were elderly, and poorly. The need to find employment became increasingly pressing for her, and so another overseas posting became unavoidable. She signed on with an agency, which required her to give them the bulk of her life savings, minimal as they were, in the hope that she'd soon be rewarded with work. On paper, the job sounded attractive: she would be sent to one of the major cities of the world to work within the diplomatic corps, albeit at its entry level: domestic. London and New York were floated as possibilities, or perhaps a return to Hong Kong; or maybe Johannesburg or Beijing; Sydney or Auckland.

She waited for months, becoming increasingly desperate, because what, in the meantime, was she supposed to live on? At last a post was found, and when it came it was urgent. If she wanted it, she'd have to move fast. She was called to the agency in Jakarta, a four-hour journey from her home, the following afternoon with bags packed. The agency would deal with the visa regulations, which meant that all that was required of her was to ensure her passport was up to date. She was to tell no one about the position, nor when she was leaving, and if all this seemed somewhat suspect to her, then desperation overrode doubt. The wages promised were good; she'd be able to send most of them back to her family to care for her daughters, and to see them educated to a level that had never been available to her.

A driver from the agency took her and another woman to the airport one dark Tuesday evening in early January, presenting them with their tickets upon arrival. Both felt excitement, and an underlying fear. They'd been told to tell Customs upon arrival that they were here on holiday, visiting friends; someone would be waiting for them. During the flight, they couldn't eat, didn't sleep, twitched and fidgeted. They arrived at dawn, and made it through passport control without query. In Arrivals, there was no one there for them.

Pavlov interjects. 'Sorry, but she told you all *this*,' he says, 'the woman so quiet we have hardly heard her voice?' He looks incredulous.

Agatha nods. 'I took her to the cafe over the bridge, the small one with the ciabattas and the profiteroles. Turns out she's rather partial to profiteroles, but then aren't we all? I told her not to worry, that she was allowed the occasional coffee break, and that it would be fine. We sat down at this tiny table, two coffees, a couple of profiteroles between us, and, honestly Pavlov, it all just came pouring out of her. The whole time she told it, there were tears streaming down her face. Her voice was entirely steady, but the tears, they wouldn't stop. It was awful, an awful thing to witness, but it was hypnotic as well, you know? She couldn't stop talking, and I couldn't stop listening. It was like bearing witness.'

At the airport they waited six hours, trying and failing to blend into their new and unfamiliar surroundings. It was cold. There were so many people. They continuously scanned the crowd in vain for signs bearing their names. At least we are together, they thought, and sat alongside each other, in silence, on hard chairs, their suitcases tucked under them. They had no money for food, for water. Their rumbling stomachs went ignored.

Six long hours passed until somebody did arrive, a man. He approached them impatiently.

'Just you,' he said, pointing at her friend. He told Lintang to wait, and when she raised her voice at him to remonstrate, he raised his back at her.

She waited a further three hours before someone else came, a man in a battered leather jacket and clutching a vape. He told her to follow him, and she practically had to run to keep up. It was by now the middle of the night. She hadn't slept since Jakarta. The car park was deserted and dark, a smell of petrol, of urine. She was terrified. She wanted to go home. They reached the car, and he told her to get in the back. She did, because what else was she to do?

He drove for over an hour, she thinks, to a large house on a main road next to a twenty-four-hour supermarket. Here she saw more men. They told her to use the bath-

109

room, and then locked her into a room which they opened only to give her food, twice a day. She stayed for three days, sleeping on and off on a single bed with a thin mattress and sheet, and had to knock for toilet breaks. Her phone had been confiscated.

Someone came to collect her, and brought her here, Agatha says, to Spring Grove.

'But get this. She has no idea where she is. She asked me whether this was the centre of town. When I told her no, that we were in the suburbs, she didn't recognise the word. This family she works for, they sound pretty dysfunctional. He's out all hours, important job, and his wife's home practically all the time. She drinks. No friends. When he *is* home, they argue, and when he's not, she sulks in the bedroom. She has long baths, and gets Lintang to scrub her back. She gets her to make her endless meals, comfort eating, probably. They've three children, all under twelve, and each of them treats Lintang badly – verbally, mostly, but occasionally phys-ically, too.

'The dogs,' she continues, 'they're a recent addition. The woman can't stand them. The man bought them for the kids after they complained he was out all the time. She has to walk them, Lintang, because the woman won't. It's the first time she's been allowed out of the house properly, in months. She still hasn't been given her phone back, and they have her passport.

'Even worse,' she says, 'they haven't paid her yet. Nothing, not a penny. She was told she'd be paid cash in hand, every week, and that she'd be able to set up a bank account here, and wire money back to the family.

She was too nervous to ask at first, but eventually she did. They kept delaying her, *next week, next week*, then they made up excuses. When she asked again, the woman hit her.

'The house is big, five bedrooms, but Lintang sleeps downstairs, in the utility room, next to the washing machine, on a mat, in a sleeping bag. She cleans from six in the morning until the woman is satisfied, which tends to be late in the evening, and long after the children have gone to bed. A lot of dust,' Agatha said, 'accumulates over four floors. Recently, they've been letting her out more, but only to take the children to school and to collect them again, and to walk the dogs. She's under strict instructions to talk to no one, and is always told to be back as soon as possible.

'And she's always home, the woman, so she's always there to check up on her, to keep tabs. She watches her like a hawk, and she's never satisfied. If you ask me, she sounds like a depressive, and she takes it all out on Lintang.'

And so Lintang lives in a perpetual state of fear. She is exhausted, in all the ways one can be. She's working without pay, a prisoner virtually, stranded thousands of miles from home. She has no idea where she is, and has neither the means to leave, nor any idea about how one may do this. She's reluctant to call the police, because she believes she is here illegally, and does not want to face either deportation or disgrace, the humiliation. Agatha did encourage her to call home, proffering her phone, but Lintang doesn't know the number. Without her phone and its contacts, they're lost to her.

'She told me that she wanted to kill herself, and that she would if it wasn't for her daughters,' Agatha says. 'She says she has these dark thoughts all the time, and these terrible tension headaches, poor thing. Migraines. She told me that she couldn't go home like this anyway, even if she wanted to, because to do so in these circumstances would bring shame on the family. And there's already shame on them because the father's left, and because she hasn't been able to send any money back.'

On the brink of tears now, Agatha stops, takes a deep breath, and shakes her head. Her sudden silence feels huge.

'But this, this is just so sad, this is terrible,' Elizabeth says quietly.

'Is slavery,' says Pavlov.

'We have to do something, we have to help,' Elizabeth says. 'We must.'

'We will.' On this, Agatha seems firm. 'We will.'

Dog walkers have a habit of inveigling themselves into all sorts of situations. This one, it seems, is mine.

Pavlov nudges me.

'Your dog,' he says, pointing.

It takes a moment to spot her. She's over on the far side of the park, at the feet of an elderly man, and I watch with slowly manifesting confusion as he stoops to attach her to a lead, then leisurely starts to walk off with her.

I run.

'Let's get you home, Norman,' I hear the man say as I draw close, and I watch as this notional *Norman* does exactly as told. Aren't dogs, I wonder, supposed to be faithful to their owners? This isn't the first time, and won't be the last, that I reconcile myself to the fact that while there is undeniably a bond between us, Missy is ultimately an amenable type, and would happily go off with anyone that bids her to. She will never stand vigil by my graveside.

'Hello?' I say, jogging alongside. The man doesn't break his stride. 'Excuse me?' I say. Now, he gives me a sidelong glance. I tell him that this is *my* dog, but the rising inflection at the end of the statement makes it sound uncertain, even to me, as if perhaps she isn't mine at all but rather *his*.

He shakes his head. 'This is Norman,' he tells me. 'It's Norman.'

The man is in his mid-seventies, upright but uncertain, an unfocused look in his eyes, an ongoing stumble to his gait. He's wearing a canvas jacket buttoned up to the neck. Alongside him, Norman glances up at me with only a cursory interest. *Not* Norman! *Missy!* If she recognises me, she makes no mention of it. She simply trots on. Judas.

'I'm afraid,' I say to him, 'that it's not Norman. I don't think you arrived with Norman today. I think you're here on your own.'

I have seen him before, this man. He walks with a Border, but older, with grey around the whiskers. Male.

'This is Missy,' I tell him. 'She's my dog, and she's a *she*.'

He falters, but only slightly, doubt beginning to implode, then looks down at her, and cranes his neck to glance between her legs. Slow mortification etches onto his features, and all of a sudden he appears on the brink of tears. This takes me by surprise, and I find that I'm almost crying, too. I apologise, as if the mistake were mine.

'Don't worry,' I say. 'Borders all look the same, pretty much, don't they?'

He makes no reply, but casts around him, trying to spot Norman, the dog who will bring sense back into the situation. There is no Norman here, not today.

I will later learn from his daughter, with whom he lives and to whom Norman belongs, that the man had been in the early stages of Alzheimer's, but that the condition is developing quickly. He's been with his daughter, a single mother, since the death of his wife a year before. They'd at first presumed his forgetfulness, and remoteness, to be a symptom of his mourning, but now his motor functions are also beginning to desert him. To mitigate this, he's become increasingly stubborn – and, his daughter tells me, he wasn't a particularly easy man before this. Insistent on maintaining his physical health, he'd taken to walking around the neighbourhood but would get lost among the newly unfamiliar shops, and the traffic that snaked its way along a perpetually clogged one-way system. His daughter had thought that walking the dog would at least confine him to the park, and it did for a while, but more and more he would leave the house alone, having forgotten him, only to find himself there alone, and confused. Police had been called on more than one occasion; the GP became involved. His daughter had started taking the dog to work with her in the hope that his absence would quell her father's roaming instincts, and also began locking him in the house. But this man who couldn't really find his way around anywhere any more had proved surprisingly adept at locating the spare key.

I tell him now that I'm heading home and that, if he wants, I can accompany him to his, first. He offers me Missy's lead with a sensitivity that squeezes at my heart, but I demur, and so the dog remains with him. We walk down a succession of streets in companionable silence, and I hope that eventually he'll lead me to his. His stiff walk does not ease, the legs not quite bending at the knee as flexibly as they should. His shoes are brown and scuffed, of a particular vintage, the laces tied in a double knot that suggests he slips in and out of them rather than troubling himself with their undoing. He continues to look squarely ahead, and I realise that there is concentration at work here, and that it should not be broken. Missy saunters alongside him obediently, the lead so tight in his left hand that the knuckles are white.

When we do reach his house, the door opens before he can find the key. He stands meekly beneath its awning as his daughter, her young son clinging to her leg, cries in frustration as she conveys the worry that this latest disappearance has caused. She scolds him for not charging his mobile phone. 'You can't go on scaring us like this, Dad,' she says. 'I'm serious, something has to change.'

I'm aware that my continued presence is helping no one, but that if I simply skulked away, I'd only make things worse. Missy, who is so shamelessly disloyal that

I briefly consider abandoning her to them, has walked into the house anyway, and is sniffing at the unfamiliar carpet. Norman comes over to meet her, two very different-looking dogs despite the similarity of the breed. Neither can conjure up much enthusiasm for the other, and so both simply sit side by side looking in opposite directions waiting for the human crisis above them to play itself out.

His daughter hugs him hard, and then, gently and with weary patience, leads him inside. She nods at me, her eyes red, and thanks me before ushering the dog back out to me, and closing the door.

When I get home, it's late. The family have eaten without me. Upon removing my phone from my pocket, I realise that it's been on silent. There are several missed calls.

The girls peer up at me. Elena looks pointedly at the wall clock.

'Should I be suspicious?' she says.

Ten

Elena takes the girls to see relatives in Spain, and I am alone for a week. It is, I think, a tacit part of any marriage contract that family events require mutually willing participants. But I don't have family any more, and since getting ill, with all its tedious consequences, I now have the perfect excuse to stay at home when she goes off to see hers. My mother-in-law does not miss me and, in truth, I've come to cherish these extended periods on my own, affording me as they do something I seem to require more and more these days: peace.

A kind of institutional madness descends when dealing with a slow and not always steady rehabilitation. In the unavoidable acceptance of my new parameters,

I have learned to acclimatise and accommodate accordingly. Where once I would have used the absence of family to immediately behave again as I had a decade earlier, going out, seeing friends, then negotiating the last bus home, I now focus on its inescapable midlife equivalent: the very real pursuit of near-total inactivity. Music becomes an uninterrupted soundtrack, and I read for hours as the outside world recedes. I forget to go shopping, and discover instead long-forgotten packets of noodles in the back of the kitchen cupboard, and hope in earnest that the soy sauce hasn't passed its sell-by date. Solitude, when temporary like this, brings a melancholy that feels distinctly pleasurable: an exercise in extreme self-centredness, while from the corner of the room Guy Garvey sings. I have nowhere to be, and nothing to do. I can come off the boil and simmer a while. Gurus might call this mindfulness. At the living-room windows, I snap shut the blinds and reach for some mood lighting.

Except of course I'm not alone now at all, not fully, not any more.

As the years of dog ownership gradually accrue, and my energy levels find and settle upon a carefully calibrated equilibrium, I'm beginning to get out more, reacquainting myself with the neighbourhood in ways I used to do before Missy arrived. In town, I stumble upon a small selection of people who offer mirror-image versions of myself much as in the park: we are folk with no more pressing places to be, all aimlessly killing time. The etiquette here *sans dog*, however, is markedly different, and I quickly revert to unsociable type.

I become a regular face amongst the three o'clock coffee drinkers, and over time establish myself at half a dozen regular haunts, where I sit in contented silence with my flat white and a book. At each place, I come to recognise the same faces, always men, always of a certain age, each with their own coffees, and each either staring into their phone screens, or else the blank patch of wall opposite. There is often at least one keen to engage, but this feels like a transgressive act within this setting, and so the rest of us shrink into our collars, and promptly turn our gaze elsewhere.

At one, in the basement of a department store that offers a perpetual sale on kitchen appliances, I learn to stealthily avoid the bonds trader who seems to operate solely from the vantage point of the cafe's most comfortable armchair, and whose seat now bears the imprint of his buttocks, two very distinct hemispheres bisected by a rising Panama Canal of pinched leather. Every time I encounter him – and I hear his voice first, rising above heads like a lugubrious bassoon – he's broadcasting financial advice to anyone foolish enough to sit anywhere near him. I am not the only one who chooses to sit as far away as possible. But then danger lurks elsewhere, too.

In the cafe's darkest corner presides the Egyptian, an elderly man with a comparably sonorous voice that chimes like church bells from two fields over. A daily presence, he is mostly consumed by the activity on his phone but there exists within him, too, this need to connect. He compliments the staff on their commitment

119

to work, comments on the quality of the coffee beans, and then casts around for other potential conversational openers. Whenever he sees me, he points me out to everyone else, and I do wish he wouldn't. He calls me The Reader.

'Aha, The Reader!' he booms, at volume. 'Every day, another book! This is wonderful, really it is. In a time of technology, this man here is keeping a dying art alive, the culture of literature, the appreciation of words on a page.' I can hear him grinning at me. 'Continue, please!'

If only it were that easy. Staying in his seat but raising his voice, impervious to the disruption he causes to everyone else, he tells me that he himself is a student of philosophy. He wants to know if I have read some of his favourite philosophers, and when I tell him that I haven't, he says, 'Pity. But no matter. One day, my friend, philosophy will come to consume you too, mark my words.' He asks if I believe in God, in the afterlife, and if he is disappointed that I answer in monosyllables, he doesn't show it.

On one occasion, there is a young man sitting between him and me. In his hand he holds a pencil, in the other, a calculator. The Egyptian appears transfixed, overjoyed.

'Well, look at what we have here! A numbers man! We have The Reader, and The Mathematician! Here! In this place of commerce and caffeine! I am greatly encouraged!'

The younger man blushes deeply, while I look quickly back down at my book. When I find my place on the page, I come across a curiously apposite paragraph, the writer explaining how, as we age, we become less concerned with socialising, and that we find others 'bewildering'. The interesting people, the writer says, are like islands. You do not encounter them by chance. You have to make the trip specially.

From the concealed speakers overhead, Neil Young sings 'Harvest Moon' in a keening croon.

'This song,' the Egyptian calls over. 'Is it Abba?'

A few times, I take Missy with me for my coffee break. This proves a mistake: it's like the circus arriving into town. Everyone looks up as I enter, the bonds trader, the Egyptian, the baristas who suddenly ignore the impatient queue in order to crouch down and stroke her. The dog removes any hopes I had of maintaining anonymity. One of the baristas tells me about her own dog back home in Bulgaria, and how much she misses him. She says that she's been here too long, and that she was supposed to return months ago but then met someone.

'It happens,' she says, shrugging despondently.

The conflict she feels at this schism in the life she otherwise imagined for herself reignites something deep within me.

It was in a cafe that I'd first encountered Elena. She had come here from somewhere else too, and had had every intention of returning home, but then we met, and she stayed. It was supposed to be a fling, but we were having so much fun together, and so many adventures. We were keen to lead full and eventful lives side by side. And we did. But all that seems a long time ago now.

I try to recall the last time we had a proper conversation, one that wasn't otherwise dominated by the routine burdens of everyday life in general. When was the last time we'd been able to enjoy ourselves without one of us reminding the other that, say, the toilet seat had broken again, or that the gutters needed emptying, the dishwasher unloading? We were living in a house that was slowly falling down, and which required our constant attention. There was a crack in the windowpane, and another on the kitchen hob that threatened electrocution every time we boiled pasta. The tiles on the roof were loose, and no longer keeping water out but rather inviting it in. The girls wanted help with their homework, or required picking up, and dropping off, putting to bed, and waking up. Their hair was always clogging the drain in the shower, and the fridge was always empty.

The two of us, then, had become by necessity a team, unified and efficient, which is as much a requirement of midlife existence as all that adventure-seeking had been for our younger selves. We do to the best of our ability everything that needs to be done, and we do so in tired tandem, either never complaining or else always complaining, depending on the day, the hour. Weeks and months run on a succession of ritual and demand, and of endless repetition: school, work, a quick dash to the supermarket, walk the dog, dinner, wine, television, a little more wine, just a bit. Highlights are few and far between. Once, we'd promised ourselves we'd go on date nights following the early years of childcare, because that's what parents do, but certain promises are hard to maintain. TV'll do. At night now, we've both taken to reading in bed, bedside lamps on, duvet drawn up to chests. We read a few chapters, then Heardle, then Wordle, then lights out, then next day: repeat. There's an impulse to say *I don't know how this happened*, but of course I do. It happens to everyone.

And it's not like we weren't expecting all this; I've read all the necessary books. Middle age is the time when everything begins to falter, and when pressures at work and at home mount. If I was the first in my immediate circle to become naggingly unwell, I wasn't the last. These days, everyone is in some or other way struggling: cancer, divorce, the lurking web of depression. Parents are beginning to pass away, old friends die from suicide. There is perimenopause and menopause, and bitter jokes about aching knees and aching backs, and migraines so bad they're surely the precursor to haemorrhage or stroke, or worse. Is there worse? As the children grow more robust and capable, the parents enter the slow decline of dependency. Life begins to feel so very, very long.

I wasn't ever really aware what an existential crisis was until I found myself in the midst of one, and whenever the family is away, I'm back in this increasingly familiar terrain. Is this depression, a midlife meltdown? If it is, I'm starting to actively counter it, in all the ways that people do: yoga, meditation, YouTube tutorials on affirmation and positivity delivered by people I'd once have crossed the road to avoid. I focus on the good, and remember just how much about my wife I still actively love: her steel and her tenacity, her kindness and her warmth, her boundless compassion. The way that, when she sneezes, she pronounces it ah-cheese. Her cooking skills, and her eagerness to read all the books I recommend which she then understands with a greater

123

intelligence than I could ever muster. The clicking noise she makes in her throat while she sleeps, which drives me mad when she does it but which I cannot quite sleep without when she's not here. Her footsteps up the stairs to bed, towards me.

Now, The Mathematician approaches me, and suddenly I'm back in the cafe. Up close, he's a little younger than I first thought, early twenties maybe. His face is open and eager. I look behind him, and see that the Egyptian has gone.

'Excuse me,' he says, 'could you keep an eye on my bag while I go to the toilet? It's just, it's got my laptop in it – and you look trustworthy.'

I raise an eyebrow.

'You're reading a book,' he says, in explanation. 'Thanks, won't be a minute.'

Later, I post an ad online: *Laptop for sale, one careful owner.*

The dog's presence during my family's occasional absences from home give my days a structure they'd otherwise lack. There are no more lie-ins, but rather an alarm clock set early. I'd be stretching the truth to suggest that I bound out of bed with enthusiasm, but not by too much. I actively *like* the fact that there is someone waiting for me, relying upon me, and whose early-morning requirements only I can fulfil. Her own enthusiasm is boundless.

The morning walkers remain largely unfamiliar to me, and the opportunity for conversation less. This suits me fine. I do my circuit, nodding to the people I cross, otherwise keeping to myself. On my first day out, I'm surprised to find that my feet are soaking. I hadn't factored in the dew, which is not an issue on the afternoon shift. I look down at my insufficient trainers – suede, old-school Gazelles, falling apart – and decide to invest in some of those all-weather walking shoes with the over-complicated design, when someone approaches.

'You're new,' she says, less a question than a statement of fact.

'I am?'

She points. 'I know her, Missy, but not you. I'm Rebecca, and this is Phoenix. Where's your wife?'

Curt, to the point. I like it. Phoenix, I soon learn, is a red Labrador, Canadian, a beauty who carries herself with the swagger of a catwalk model. She and Missy tease each other with teeth, while Rebecca astonishes me by unfolding what soon comes to feel like her entire biography before eight o'clock in the morning. In doing so, she transgresses the early walkers' code of conduct, and I am trapped. She appears in no rush at all. She tells me that she is a forty-two-year-old marketing executive mother of two, and that she is soon to separate from a husband whom she hasn't yet told.

'He's an ageing graffiti artist,' she says, 'and a crypto currency obsessive.'

I must do something with my face here, because now she's looking at me more quizzically.

'You've met him?'

I admit that I have. 'But he walks a spaniel, no?'

'Peter, yes. Peter's his, Phoenix's mine. He's made that very clear. Separate dogs, separate walks.' She laughs dryly. 'And I married this man. People change, you know?'

She tells me that her dream is to escape, and to travel, and she imparts all this with such yearning I'm half tempted to ask if I can come.

'I want to see Vietnam and Laos, Cambodia, anywhere thousands of miles from here.'

When I tell her I've been to one of those countries, she's hungry for details, then calls up images on her phone to satisfy herself with visuals. Rebecca has jet-black hair and high cheekbones, she wears skinny jeans and bright white trainers, and looks like she takes physical fitness seriously. I realise that it would be accurate to say that she complements her dog in much the way Sid complements Rocky. It's been a long time since I've had a conversation like this, and so it takes me a while to recognise that, in constantly flicking her hair over one shoulder and laughing at everything I say, she might be flirting. This seems highly improbable to me, and yet.

'You're funny,' she says, smiling.

The moment passes, and I'm a little relieved for it, when we're joined by another woman. This one I do recognise. Her black poodle is another Coco. In her telling, Coco and Missy had struck up an early friendship as puppies, and so are therefore forever friends. I don't know the owner's name, but she's a nervous person, eyes darting while she talks, as if constantly surveying the place for near and present danger. This morning, her hair is in a high ponytail, and she's wearing an oversized sweatshirt that reads I DON'T EVEN LIKE THE PEOPLE I LIKE. She begins to tell us about a recent dog attack, and the need for extra vigilance. She refers to Coco's multiple health issues, and how they seem to align in tandem with hers. It's when she says the words 'anal glands' that Rebecca glances very deliberately at her watch, the kind that monitors heart rate, steps and mood. I watch her tap it with the tip of her index finger. Manicured nails. It lights up, and winks at her.

'Nice meeting you,' she says. 'See you next time, perhaps?'

When I get home, whim dictates that I shave and spruce myself up a bit. Can't hurt.

The first time we go on our annual summer holiday after getting the dog, none of us feels quite ready to leave her behind with strangers, and so we pack her, figuratively, with the suncream. For convenience, we choose the country closest to ours, which means we don't have to fly. We drive. It takes seven hours. She sits upright all the way, panting.

The destination is a holiday camp, our first. We stop en route for lunch, but the city's many parks each boast signs that read No Dogs, and warn of heavy fines for those that don't clean up after their animals. And so our three-hour stroll up and down its pretty boulevards comes increasingly to resemble torture, nowhere for her to relieve herself when that is precisely what she needs to do. When finally she does give in to bodily requirement, in the middle of crossing a busy road while the traffic light is only fleetingly green for us, I can hardly blame her. The lights change just as she finishes, and the oncoming cars mean that I have to leave it where it fell, and run for the nearest kerb. When, a moment later, a truck flattens her shit into a pancake, three people at the pavement cafe opposite stand to cheer and applaud.

The campsite is dog-friendly, but requires pets to remain on a lead at all times. The playground and the swimming pool are out of bounds, which means that one of us needs to remain behind with her, or else she howls. She barks incessantly at cows in the neighbouring field, then later barks frenziedly at a life-size carbon-fibre cow outside a steak restaurant, causing several small children nearby to jump in fear, and the manager to ask us to leave.

She gets ticks, three fat, grey and perfectly spherical things that attach themselves to her neck, chin and vulnerable belly. Each becomes swollen with her blood, and we've no idea how to get them off her. The vet is lugubrious, and seems terribly bored by life as he tells us that the ticks might make her sick for the rest of her life.

'It is difficult to say,' he says with a shrug I take to be typically Gallic. 'You must wait and see.'

The dog is clearly relieved to be home a few days after. Finally, an environment that she understands, and is allowed to wander around at will. Within minutes of walking through the front door, to a mountain of mail and a cooped, musty smell, she collapses into her corner of the sofa, and refuses to move for the next twelve hours.

'Never again,' Elena says.

The following year, dog sitters.

Eleven

Olivia runs wildly towards me, grinning, although from this distance it's hard to be sure. Perhaps it's a grimace, perhaps she's in pain? With Olivia, it often tends towards one extreme or the other. Halfway over, she reduces speed and moves into slow motion, exaggerating the piston movements of both arms, and elaborately tossing her head from side to side in the manner of a Californian lifeguard.

'Have you heard?' she says, and, not waiting for my answer, proceeds to tell me all about Lintang, both the ongoing situation *and* the group's developing intention to try and do something about it. I experience an undeniable thrill here. I'm part of the gang, *included*. It's like being back at school, a playground huddle. As she talks, she places the palm of her right hand against her forehead as if testing for fever, or else to push back all the turbulent thoughts pressing in her mind.

'Are you in?' she asks.

I nod eagerly, and suddenly I'm lost within an embrace I didn't see coming.

'Wonderful!' she says. 'Excellent!'

Olivia, the actor, is in her mid-twenties, cis, all the usual pronouns. I occasionally see her walking her family's red setter here, and she always seems to be in preparation for an upcoming audition, not all of which she successfully lands. I've often observed her here striding back and forth across the grass, skittish as a deer, while reciting her lines at volume. Her dog follows faithfully behind, nose to the ground.

'I know what you're thinking,' she says. 'It all screams of liberal guilt, and, right, *right*, I get that, I do. Because how on earth are we – *us!* – in a position to actually really properly help? But we have to do *something*, right? We have to at least *try*.'

It is Olivia, over the next few days, who strives to poke her nose in furthest, further even than Agatha. 'It's the actress in me,' she says, insisting that she was named after Sir Laurence. She clearly likes to perform, and loves an audience. Life's her stage. In any delicate situation where, in order to really help, one has to be unselfconsciously bullish and take control, it's she, Olivia, who emerges as the optimum, the only, candidate here. Even Agatha defers to her.

'I'm your man,' she says. 'I'll talk to Lintang some

more; we live on the same road. I see her putting the bins out. I'll talk to her, and tell her that we can help, and then we'll work out the practicalities afterwards. How does that sound?'

Everyone agrees.

Her setter has the curious misfortune of a constant erection. He has one now, and while Olivia chatters on, he is a few feet away, dragging his hindquarters across the grass, a rictus grin on his long boyish face. Olivia notices, and blushes.

'Poor thing. He'll hump anything, any*one*, come to think of it. So stand back. He can't help himself, it's a condition.'

Olivia is several years out of drama school, but the big break is still pending. For three months last winter, she was in the chorus line of *Les Misérables*, and has been part of a performing theatrical group in Kerala, from which she returned with both fond memories *and* botulism. She has exotic, tumbledown auburn hair, and the kind of arresting features – big eyes, high cheekbones, good teeth – that look striking from every angle.

'The camera *loves* me,' is something she very much likes to say.

Currently, she's part of a small troupe of actors who put on private performances in people's homes. She is actively pursuing bookings.

'Let's say you're having a dinner party,' she once explained, 'and twenty people are invited. Well, after dessert, we put on a forty-five-minute play, right there in your living room, in the *round*. It's amazingly intimate. You should hire us! No, please, I'm serious. *Do*. Tell your friends!'

131

She's been an extra in TV shows, playing a shop-keeper, a stallholder, a passerby and a dancer in a nightclub. She's been three dead bodies in TV police procedurals, one of them Swedish, and two nurses with non-speaking roles in daytime hospital dramas. She can sing and dance, and ride horses bareback, but hasn't yet passed her driving test. She has *carpe diem* tattooed in ornate curlicues on one arm, and a question mark on her left hip, which she once showed to Pavlov, and laughed when his cheeks turned crimson. She can quote long-dead Chinese philosophers, but none of the living ones.

About a month ago, I saw her march through the park without her dog, crying hysterically.

'*Don't even,*' she said, holding up a hand emphatically enough to stop traffic, after I'd approached her, concerned.

She's back living at home now where her mother has had a breakdown and refuses to get out of bed. Her father is quietly nursing an alcohol problem far less quietly than he imagines. She is terrified of turning thirty, and doesn't want anyone mentioning the actor Florence Pugh within earshot.

A week passes.

The afternoon dog walk has now become something else entirely, the dogs still present but left mostly unattended to do their own thing. There are no complaints. Among us all there is much discussion of what to do, and I'm intrigued by how sure of themselves everyone seems to be. I always thought I was a fairly proactive individual – as a freelancer, you rather have to be: work won't come to find *me* if I don't search tirelessly for *it* – but it turns out I'm entirely passive, part of the flock. The humdrum of everyday life has suddenly developed, of all things, both plot *and* narrative, and my fellow walkers are clambering over one another to snag a leading role. The atmosphere fairly crackles. Some of the conversations are now faintly comical, and it's clear that while we have good intent, we have no idea what we can actually do, and little conception of how to agree on anything. But the purpose at least remains a serious one, and in this Olivia's in the role of her life.

'She's desperate, Lintang,' Olivia says, 'and I think you're right, Agatha, she might be . . . well, vulnerable too. So whatever we do decide to do, it has to be quick.'

Elizabeth is particularly keen that we settle upon affirmative action. 'So what *shall* we do?' she asks.

Olivia touches her tattoo, *carpe diem*. 'No police, no authorities. She's terrified of both. I think we just need to get her out of there, that house,' she says.

She stares off into the middle distance, and I can't help but wonder if she's been bidden to do so by an unseen director. It's true, I realise, that some people require constant drama in their lives, and if it's absent, then they find it – create it themselves, even. During the summer months, Olivia does aerobics in the park dressed in a bright blue leotard, no shoes. The red setter accompanies her. She invites passers-by to join in. Some do.

'Here's what I think,' she says. 'This is what we have to do: force the issue because *she* won't. Stage an intervention, of sorts. We did something similar with my mother once. For different reasons, admittedly, but with the same outcome hopefully: a resolution. If she's too scared to run away by herself – and she has every right to be: she's far from home, no phone, no passport, no money, *alone* – then it has to be us that helps get her somewhere safe.'

A chorus of: 'Yes, but *where?*'

'Working on it.'

Over the next couple of weeks, Olivia times her afternoon walks to coincide with Lintang's. 'Research,' she calls it. They meet halfway down the street, nodding subtly at one another without breaking stride. The moment they're safely out of view of the house, Lintang begins to talk. As they walk together, Olivia does what no one has done for Lintang for a long time now: she listens.

'It's the strangest thing,' she says, 'it all just pours out of her.'

Agatha nods eagerly. 'Yes,' she says. 'She was like that with me, too.'

Olivia continues. 'I feel like her psychotherapist, like she's been storing all this . . . this stuff up, and it just needs to come out. The things that poor woman has gone through.'

During the previous twenty years, Lintang has only spent a few months back home. She'd had her children young, a casual fling suddenly requiring the presumed solidity of marriage when she found herself pregnant. Her husband was cruel and selfish, a drinker and gambler, and would routinely disappear for weeks at a time. Her girls still toddlers, she left him and moved back in with her parents, and in time sought work overseas when money became an issue. This would require her leaving them behind for many months at a time.

In Riyadh, she worked for a German businessman and his wife, on the twenty-seventh floor of an apartment that boasted far-reaching views of the skyscraper city, and the desert beyond. The couple were childless and preoccupied, and easily ignored her as she went about her work, entering rooms only when she knew them to be empty. The work was hard, but the pay decent, and she sent most of it back home. Six months in, and with the wife away on business, the man abruptly decided to take notice of his cleaner, and insisted she stop what she was doing and give him a massage instead. He was feeling tense, he told her. Who knows, he added, she might enjoy it too?

Lintang had been trained to obey, and so when she entered his bedroom a few minutes later to find him lying face down on the mattress, naked, she recoiled, but did not leave. He was a heavy and, as it transpired, hirsute man, his back covered with long black hairs, like a bear. He pointed out the baby oil on the bedside table, and encouraged her to follow his instructions.

'Things developed from there,' Olivia relayed. The man turned over to expose himself, and Lintang fled, running to the kitchen, her back up against the wall, while wielding a bread knife. In a quiet voice, she told him she would use it.

'The man screamed at her to get out,' Olivia said. 'Fired her.'

*

Over the years she made friends and acquaintances, colleagues she'd encounter in various postings. Most, like her, were live-in domestics working six-day weeks. On the seventh, a Sunday, they'd congregate in parks and on public benches, exchanging gossip, sharing food, and conveying respective hardships. Some had been trafficked into sex work, others found that sex was as much a requirement as the ironing. Each of them felt bound to their employers through fear, and the overriding need to send money home. Lintang's awareness of world events and daily news was limited but she knew all about the Jungle in Calais, the asylum seekers in Lampedusa, the refugee camps on former RAF bases in England. She knew that several of her friends, for various reasons, had ended up in such places, and she knew, too, that some had made money, and *had* returned home with their savings, a notionally happy ending. This was always the ultimate aim, the thing that kept all of them going: the possibility, however vague, that they could return home prosperous.

'I just want to provide for my family, for my daughters,' she told Olivia. 'I want them to have a better life than I have had.'

Olivia asked her what she desired for herself. 'What do *you* want?' she said.

Lintang was silent for a moment, thinking.

'My freedom,' she said.

It becomes known as 'the plan', and is mentioned in such a way that you can almost hear the quotation marks. The plan is simple in its intent: there's to be a whip-round.

'Of course,' Olivia says, 'money is not the answer to Lintang's problems, but if we can at least raise some money for her, then it will facilitate her escape, and give her some short-term options. She can leave Spring Grove in the knowledge that she won't, at least, be homeless. And then she can plan her next move.

'But first we have to help her escape. They've confiscated her passport, but it must be in the house somewhere. She won't leave without it, because without it she's a ghost, a non-person. So we'll get it back for her. We'll wait until the house is empty, Lintang can let us in, we find it, and then she goes. Simple.'

Afterwards, Pavlov tells me that sometimes he observes the actions of the younger generation and feels not only envy, and perhaps a little jealousy, but also a reeling admiration.

'The young,' he says, 'they believe that everything is possible, even when is not. But then this is how revolution happens, big and small. Because let me tell you, in that moment, when Olivia talks about breaking and entering, I fall in love with her. I fall for the, the – you know – the pure radiance of her, this shining light, this beautiful madness. For me, she lives in the cloud and the cuckoo land, but for her is reality because she will make it so. Me, I would not be able to do what she is doing. I am old, and I can only see faults in this plan; I can only anticipate all the things that could go wrong – and, if you ask me, *will* go wrong. But Olivia? No! To her, all is potential. She sees opportunity everywhere. This I admire.'

He says that he cannot understand why she is not a famous actress yet.

'Me, I buy every word that comes from her mouth!'

Olivia finishes her speech, the proposal parcelled up and delivered to each of us. She opens her eyes wide.

'So, what do you think?'

Agatha nods firmly. 'Yes, yes. It's perfect.'

The affirmation rings in the air, and our tight circle grows tighter still. Benji ambles by, asking whether anyone has seen his shoes, but Agatha doesn't break eye contact with Olivia.

'When?' she wants to know.

'Soon, soon.'

Twelve

Into the argument comes only silence, and then the whirring intestinal noise the fridge likes to make when it thinks no one is listening. I have never been one to storm out of rooms, or to slam doors – too much of that in my childhood – but I do now call the dog more sharply than I normally would, harness her with a certain impatience, then stalk off down the cold pavement towards the park, Missy somewhat bewildered but by no means put out by the fact that we've already had our afternoon walk, just an hour previously. A reliable creature of habit, she stops to smell the same cracks in the road on the way, and pees against the same creeping vines on the same garden wall, and I envy her certitude, the fact that everything in life is as it should be, and that, given the choice, she probably wouldn't wish to improve upon anything at all.

The argument was nothing out of the ordinary, just more daily frustrations that had been simmering a while, and which needed occasionally to rise to the surface. These were times when I realised, regrettably late, just how much my new circumstances were affecting my wife, too. I'd always been adamant that my downturn in health shouldn't limit her life as it had mine, and I encouraged her to keep active, and social, and busy. This she does, no longer as part of a pair but rather mostly alone, having to make excuses for me as I grow increasingly predictable in my absence. She's in mourning for the couple we used to be. I am too, because while she is out there, living, I'm stuck stewing here, at home. I always grew easily bored at home, allergic to cabin fever, quick to crave further outdoor adventure. I never used to be a hermit. Throughout the early part of our relationship, it had been *she* who had to run to keep up with *me*. Not any more.

The fresh air provides an instant balm, an anaesthetic. I pass the post office sorting depot where, once again, postal workers are out on strike, clad in their pink bibs, and waving hand-written banners towards traffic in the hope that drivers will honk their horns in a show of solidarity. Some of them look as downtrodden as I currently feel, which offers a curious relief. The dog walks past them with wilful indifference and leads me to the park. Acting more on instinct than probable need, she squeezes out her third number two since breakfast, then looks around at me and cocks her head as if to say, 'And now?'

Seeing something, or some*one*, off she goes with sudden impetus, tail wagging. I look up, and follow her trail. I've not seen him for at least a week now, but here he is, the bald head, the sheepskin collar, the piratical gait, and immediately I feel relief: an ally when I most need one. He offers me the upward tilt of his chin as he approaches, while an accompanying grimace indicates the pain he must surely feel but which he won't discuss.

'Pavlov, good to see you.'

'Hello, my friend. I haven't seen you around for a bit, where you been?'

I confess that I've been cheating on him with another park recently, this one by the school that tends to get overcrowded after three with milling children. The dog walkers here are more the loner type, which means I'm left mercifully alone. I tell him that I've been going through some things, and had simply craved a change of scenery.

'I just wanted to be on my own for a bit,' I tell him, surprised by the sensation that comes with this admission, that I've slighted him somehow.

He laughs dryly. 'My friend, I have been there,' he says, though whether he means this figuratively or literally, I can't quite tell. To the best of my knowledge, Pavlov and Dog have never been to any park but this one, it being the furthest distance he can walk without his hip becoming unbearable. If my own horizons have shrunk these past few years, his have shrunk more.

'Trouble at home?' he asks.

'Trouble up here,' I say, tapping my head. To this he nods.

141

I'm still not particularly good at talking about myself, of making myself the centre of the conversation. My instinct is to deflect, and to turn the tables. It's a condition of my job, perhaps: the ability to ask searching questions that encourages revealing answers, while I keep mostly quiet and nod sagely. But there is another reason for my reticence, I think. I'm fearful of others' response, and the buzz kill I elicit as a result. People only like to talk about their own misery; they don't want to hear about the misery of others. And so now I only vaguely tell Pavlov what's up, how my mood is impacting the family unit, and the toll it takes on my wife who, for so much of the time, endures it all with such empathy and grace. Those doctors I saw early on would tell me that they looked for signs of depression in me but could never find it. Perhaps they could find it now.

I quickly grow tired of the sound of my own voice, and instead say: 'Anyway, Pavlov, how's things with you?' in the hope that his inevitably lengthy answer will drown out every last lingering thought in my head.

'Let me tell you something,' he says, and I think: *here we go*. 'Midlife, and getting older, it can be illustrated, I think, in this way. Picture a room, big room with lots of doors. The doors are all open, yes? That's youth. But over time, one by one, they close. Some they close so quietly you don't notice; others they slam shut in your face. And so your job now? Your job is to find the one that's still open, and make it maximum comfort for yourself.'

He smiles at me, and pats me on my back, but then he trips on an uneven patch of grass and almost falls, something he's keen to avoid at his age and in his condition. I reach out to him, and help him right himself, and witness a wince of pain that forces his eyes tight shut. Inwardly, I smile wryly, because in the space of a couple of minutes we have both propped the other up. There must be a metaphor here somewhere.

'I'm fine, I'm fine,' he says impatiently, and before I can stop him, or direct the conversation elsewhere, he's telling me about his mother.

'My mother,' he says, 'when we are back in Russia, she did not have the most original line in thought, is true, but she keep telling me how we are born alone and we die alone, and that most we can hope for while alive is for a truthful companionship that will last as long as we need it to. Her husband – my father, you know – he left when I was twelve, and for her that is enough, men no more. She gets what she need, and she didn't need to go back for more with another man. Was she happy afterwards? No, she was miserable! She was Russian! But like I say, is life.'

Suddenly distracted, he looks up.

'Hello, Agatha, hello Elizabeth!'

We shift our stance to accommodate them.

'I am just telling Nick here,' he says, 'about the meaning of life.' He laughs, and Agatha frowns. 'I am telling him that there comes a point when we do not need our relationships to continue. They become too broken, too painful to maintain, and unnecessary, and we see that we are better alone.'

Agatha's eyebrows rocket up her forehead, wiping clean her frown as they go. 'What the hell are you talking about, Pavlov?' she says. 'Are you trying to ruin Nick's life?' She pulls me away from him as if distance is what's required.

He reiterates his point, using much the same words in much the same order, but employs more adjectives now to appear more declarative. I notice a thick vein beginning to pulse at his left temple. Being challenged gets his blood up. Over his left shoulder, the sun is beginning to set.

'We become tired,' he says in conclusion, 'and we become accustomed to disappointment. Life is long, no? Better to uncomplicate it, then. How? I tell you how. We become,' he smiles, 'islands in the stream.'

Now Agatha laughs. 'Dolly Parton?'

'You, Agatha, perhaps, yes. Me? Kenny Rogers.'

I think I see something pass between them, and look down at Elizabeth for confirmation, who appears entirely confused by the exchange.

'Listen, I give you example,' he says, ignoring Agatha's eye roll. 'My last girlfriend. We are good together, and I think to myself: at last! We both suffer before, and we both carry the scars, you know? We met, this was online, and we talked and we liked each other, same experiences, same attitude. No children, no parents, both love dogs. We get together, and for a time is us against the world, just like in the films! She says she loves me and wants to live with me, and I think to myself, okay, okay, why not? So she moves in. But then she changes, you know? Not immediately, but soon enough. She has these habits, these things she likes to do in particular way. Like OCD. Yes, yes, I like to do things my own way too, but trouble is mine is *different* way, not like hers. And so, hey presto, we are no longer compatible, we do not fit together no more. And is more than just leaving toilet seat up or down, okay? We are set in our ways, and no one wants to change, nor compromise.'

'So you left her?' Agatha asks.

Pavlov immediately blushes hard. It's like watching red paint thrown across a white canvas. 'Well, yes,' he begins, 'I was going to, but she leaves me first. This was Christmas. She tells me that she has become mortally disappointed in me. This is the word she uses: *mortally*. She tells me that she could die if she have to spend another Christmas with me. She exaggerates a lot, I think. Anyway, this was going to be our third Christmas together, and on December twenty-second, she just leaves. Was I sad? Sure, very! But like I say, is life. I had Dog by then, still with four legs, he didn't disappoint me, he didn't let me down, he didn't leave. No. We respect each other's differences, I don't want him to change, he doesn't want me to change, we rub the right way. So this is it for me now, enough, no more. I'm old.'

He looks penetratingly at Agatha. 'But you agree with me, Agatha, yes? I mean, because you are alone too, Elizabeth also. So many of us here in the park – this I say to Nick already, before – with our dogs every day, we are alone. Why is this? Coincidence? I think not.'

'No!' she says hotly. 'No! I do not agree with you, Pavlov. Me, I *want* companionship, I *want* love. I want another human heart beating next to mine when I fall asleep at night, and when I wake up in the morning. And I'm endlessly optimistic I'll find it again one day, because if I don't have hope, then what *do* I have? I refuse to believe that on a planet that has however many millions and millions of people—'

'Eight point one billion,' Pavlov says authoritatively.

'Eight billion people, whatever. I refuse to believe that there isn't *one* person out there for *me*. No, I may not have found him yet, but I have found some, and they were good while they lasted, and I loved them, and they me. I'd also argue, Pavlov, that we become *more* accepting of our differences as we age, not *less*. When we get older, we don't just want infatuation and passion, and lust and dancing all night – although, speaking personally, I'm still very much for all that, thanks – we also want quiet companionship, someone to sit at the kitchen table with, to make us tea, or to crash out with in front of the TV. I want to meet someone, fall in love, go on holiday, and also just to wander up and down the high street with on a Saturday morning, to split a croissant with at the cafe, and to hold hands with right here in the park while we walk the dog. I want someone who accepts me with all my flaws, and my scars, just as I'll accept them. Pavlov, the world is filled with the most wonderful people, the kindest, the gentlest souls. You just have to be open to them, and ready to accept them. Not everyone has an agenda, not everyone is cruel, or nasty, or selfish. You, Pavlov,' and she's pointing now, '*you* can dwell on the negative if you want, but me? I'll embrace optimism, I'll embrace hope. Just because *your* romantic life hasn't quite panned out as you'd hoped, doesn't mean that it might not yet still, one day.'

It's only when she stops talking that I realise how loud her voice was. The silence proves quite the contrast.

Pavlov coughs into his fist, and natural colour comes gradually back into his cheeks. If I'm not mistaken, he's beginning to look emboldened, somehow.

'So, Agatha, would *you* go out on a date with me?'

She laughs.

'I'm serious.'

'Are you?'

'Why not?' he says, first shrugging, then offering up a smile I've not seen on his face before.

Elizabeth, who had been mutely attentive, now takes a step forward.

'When my husband died, I was thirty-nine years old,' she says. 'I've been alone ever since. I have raised two daughters. They've grown up and gone out into the world, and it's just me and Betty now. In many ways, I had a frustrating marriage, not always a very happy one. He was older than me by thirteen years, a different generation almost. He didn't say very much, he just sort of brooded, kept things to himself. He was carrying things, I think, these heavy thoughts, from the war perhaps, or from his upbringing, or maybe it was just the era he was born into? He was the only man I've ever known, and even though he could drive me mad sometimes, and he really did, he was my partner in life, he gave me my girls. We didn't really have very many expectations of each other, I don't think. We got married, and it was what it was, but I loved him with my very being. He died of lung cancer when he was fifty-two – he'd been a heavy smoker, you know – and I don't think I've ever stopped mourning him, really. I talk to him every day still. If you saw me around the house, you'd think me mad, talking out loud to myself, or maybe to Betty, and I *am* talking to Betty sometimes, but mostly, do you know, I'm talking to him, to my husband, telling him all the things I never got to tell him when I had the chance. And do you want to know what the funny thing is? He listens. He listens, and he answers me, and so he's still here with me. And that's enough for me, it is.'

Pausing to take a breath, Elizabeth looks sheepish, as if surprised by having spoken out. She normally doesn't.

'People today,' she continues, 'they have higher expectations, more demands. They want to be happy all the time, and I can't say I blame them. But I can't help but worry that the pursuit of all this happiness is ultimately making them disappointed, and sad. Everyone wants to measure up to everybody else, but no one is being entirely honest. I see a lot of sadness around here, and Pavlov's right, I see a lot of people all by themselves, and sometimes I just want to go up to them and hug them. That would be inappropriate of me, of course, and so I don't, but I do wish I could help, help to alleviate their suffering somehow.'

'But you do!' Agatha tells her.

'I do?'

'You do, just by being you,' she says. 'And you can give me a cuddle whenever you like!'

'In Russia,' Pavlov says, 'we have a saying: Нет худа без добра.'

He looks around at each of us, waiting for someone to take the bait. Agatha does.

'Which means?'

'It means that there is no good without bad. So take, for

example, me, my situation. I'm alone, yes? My leg, it gives me pain. I have no hair left, and not just on my head,' Agatha winces, 'and I haven't had sex in almost six years,' Agatha winces again, 'and my work has pretty much gone. I'm living on disability benefits, I don't go out much. But still I am here every day, in park, with Dog, who I love more than life itself, and who keeps me alive. Here, I have the trees, and the fresh air. And I have you. I have my daily conversations with each of you, which, yes, even you, Agatha, means more to me than I can ever say.'

I can see that Agatha wasn't expecting this. She smiles as Pavlov rubs his eyes.

'Is true,' he stresses. 'All of you, you are my community now, my family almost. I don't have one outside this park, and I am okay with that now, I am. I get everything I need from this, from you, from here. I get my exercise, I get to talk, and you all kindly listen. And do you know what? If anything has restored my faith in people, in humanity, and in the world, at least a little bit, is this. Is you! All of you! You remind me that, okay, the world isn't that bad. If I'm feeling sad at home, and I come here to meet you, then I go back home feeling little bit better. Not always by very much, is true,' he adds, laughing, and looking pointedly at Agatha again, 'but definitely less sad. I think we show each other kindness here, we understand each other, more or less, in ways that don't always need to be expressed . . . Except, of course, that I am expressing it now.'

He blushes deeply once more. 'So thank you,' he says.

'Pavlov, you're not trying to make us cry, are you?' Agatha says, returning his impish grin.

'I am not,' he confirms.

'Good!' She sighs out loud. 'If I'd known we were going to be getting in quite so deep today, and for quite so long, I'd have worn more comfortable shoes.'

Elizabeth clutches onto her arm, and laughs. 'Look who's coming,' she says. Up ahead, Olivia is approaching. Before she arrives into the circle, Pavlov becomes sombre again.

'Listen, Nick,' he tells me, 'don't forsake what you have at home, you understand me? You still got good family, and good wife, a *good* wife, and if I am honest with you I would trade with you in one single heartbeat. In Russia, we would call Elena а хорошая жена.'

I ask for a translation, and he looks at me like I'm slow.

'A good wife!'

'Hey, hi, hello,' Olivia says, beaming. 'What's happened, who died? You all look so terribly serious!'

'Pavlov has been telling us his version of the meaning of life,' Agatha says.

Olivia nods knowingly, then opens up her arms into an embrace each of us fails to walk into, even Elizabeth. 'Hug it out!' Olivia laughs.

'Right,' Elizabeth says, 'let's walk, shall we? I came here for some exercise, not to get all maudlin.'

Together, we do three more circuits, and the conversation settles into something more accommodatingly routine. Elizabeth tells of a promotion her daughter got recently, and says that in order to maintain a relationship with her grandchildren, who grow so quickly, every week a little taller, a little more grown-up, she Zooms with them after her breakfast and their dinner.

'I've got it on the laptop, you know,' she explains. 'The *app*.'

'I do not trust Zoom,' Pavlov says, adding, as if in explanation: 'technology.'

Agatha taps me on the arm, and points. I turn to look, and see Elena, wrapped up in her coat and scarf, smiling warmly as she approaches. She looks radiant. It's late, *I'm* late, and she's come to fetch me. When she reaches me, she kisses my cheek. A silent exchange passes between us, carried by a freighted look that communicates much of what we'd both wanted to say earlier but didn't, couldn't.

'We've just been talking about you,' Pavlov says.

She frowns. 'Oh, really?'

'Not really, we weren't,' says Agatha. 'Pavlov was just dismantling the many mysteries of life for us, and your name came up briefly, that's all.'

'Should I have got here sooner, then?' Elena wonders.

'Oh, don't encourage him! I think we've all heard enough from Pavlov for one day.' Agatha glances down at her dog, who, for once, she has permitted to walk rather than be carried. 'Time to get you home,' she tells him. 'Dinner.'

Elena links her arm with mine. We say our goodbyes to the group, leaving the remaining walkers to decide upon an additional, and final circuit.

'I had the most amazing dream last night,' I hear Olivia tell them.

'What was it about?' Elizabeth asks encouragingly.

'Oh, *so* many things!'

151

Thirteen

I find myself drawn to Spring Grove almost daily now, making it a routine part of my walk home and intrigued by the slowly unfolding drama that takes place there. I can't help but admire the house's Gothic bearing, looming over the corner of its part of the road like an admonishing headmaster, and I'm aware that I crave some kind of minor incident from it as I pass, someone at the window, perhaps, or a door being flung open dramatically, raised voices; *evidence*.

I only realise now, with a jolt of recognition I should perhaps have felt weeks ago, the house's number: 11. Viv the dog psychic had told me that a door with the number 11 would become significant to me, and now here I am.

If Missy is aware of my belated recognition, a canine *told you so*, she fails to show it. Olivia lives in one of the smaller houses on the street, and has over the past few weeks wormed herself into Lintang's trust with a sense of affection that has partially becalmed the other woman's distress. In Olivia, she has at last a confidante in this country so far from home. She knows that a group of us are planning to help her escape, and Olivia has told us that she, Lintang, is open to the idea, but nevertheless remains a little uncertain, and afraid. To go along with this will not be easy for her, but then when you've lived for so long in fear, bravery does not suddenly assert itself. This isn't a movie.

But it *is* a drama, and it keeps this motley crew, of which I am somehow a part, unambiguously energised. Over the last few days, each of us has been cursed by group dynamics. I tend to watch mostly from the sidelines as Agatha and Olivia battle it out for, appropriately, top-dog status. Both are dominant and proactive, fuelled with a vicarious sense of injustice, and a strong need to be the architects of its dismantling. I would have expected Pavlov to challenge them, but Pavlov has grown unaccountably meek in their company, and simply listens to their scheming with as much silent interest as I do. We are equals at last. Elizabeth is comparably quiet, and craves only a happy resolution with the minimum of upheaval for the innocent whom she cannot think of without welling up.

Olivia remains the conduit. They walk together now every day under the veil of an innocent dog walk, and this helps, Olivia says, maintain the confidence Lintang will require to see it through. Regardless, there is currently more talk than action. Each afternoon I arrive at the park anticipating progress; we all do, patience a virtue we lack.

In the meantime, Olivia gathers information. The husband is out every day from early morning, and not back until dark. He gets home tired, hungry, and in no mood to tolerate noise from the children, no matter how excited they might be to see him. The children are at school between nine and three, then homework until 5.30 p.m. The wife is at home most days, tauntingly unemployed, where she lingers long in bed for want of anything better to do, invariably in front of the television whose channel she changes frequently in pursuit of lasting distraction. There are only ever guests at the house in the evening, and these tend to be the husband's colleagues, and mostly men, during which time Lintang is expected to cook, serve, light cigarettes and wash up after, irrespective of the hour. The wife's morning-after hangovers are redolent of depression, and Lintang has grown to be wary of them. She hoovers only downstairs until the wife has emerged from her room to face the day, unsettled and mostly sad. She often chooses to wallow in her daily bath with its bubbles and its fragrances, intermittently calling Lintang in to top it up with hot water, and to scrub her back with a sponge sourced from the deep waters of Central America. Lintang has told Olivia that the wife craves company and that, in different circumstances, might have reached out to Lintang as an ally, a friend even. But the only arrangement available is the one both find themselves in: each trapped inside lives they'd not quite foreseen. Neither is happy. She cooks the wife a different lunch each day, sourced by the latter from recipes she finds online. Most afternoons, at least during the warmer months, Lintang is directed to the garden to tend to the lawn and the flower beds. At three, she collects the children from school; at four, she walks the dogs. At five, while overseeing their homework, she begins preparation for the children's dinner, and again at eight for the parents'. In this way, weeks go by, and then months.

It's on Thursday afternoons that the wife gets dressed to go out, and leaves the house for an extended period of time. Lintang has no idea where she goes, but thinks it might be a weekly appointment at the hairdresser or beauty salon, and then perhaps a browse through the shops afterwards. Whatever it is that she does do, she's gone from one o'clock until shortly after three: a window of two hours. Previously during these times, Lintang has slept, grateful for the temporary oblivion, waking only for the school run.

I'm in the park one afternoon with Agatha when she and Olivia arrive unexpectedly early. Agatha tells her to stay awake this week.

'Not this week,' Lintang tells her.

Agatha asks why.

'There is a dinner party in the evening. I have to cook.'

'How does that matter? You'll be gone! Let them fend for themselves!'

But Lintang remains firm. 'It does matter,' she says. 'The food is ordered, and there is a lot of it. People are coming. The wife is anxious. She's relying on me. I must.'

Agatha bites her tongue, and shrugs her shoulders.

'Next week, then?' Olivia suggests.

Lintang starts to nod but then stops, and then changes her mind, and nods with more determination. 'Yes,' she says. More loudly now, she says it again. '*Yes.*'

She looks in no way prepared for what will happen next.

One of us buys a large padded envelope, into which we each deposit some money. Agatha puts in three twenties, I put in thirty, Elizabeth fifteen. Sid offers ten. Pavlov stuffs in fifty, money he can't afford, but he remains insistent. 'A good cause,' he says. Olivia, in a break from the agreed confidentiality between us all, has told her parents about it. Her mother was shocked and horrified, and is intent on writing a letter to her local MP to raise the issue of slave labour in the neighbourhood. She has given two hundred. It seems that Agatha has done similar within the school staffroom at work. The envelope is overflowing.

'It's still not very much,' Agatha says, 'but it's something. It's a start.'

She seals the envelope and, with a pen she removes from one of the many pockets of her cargo trousers, writes the name Lintang, in purple felt tip, on the front.

And then, quite suddenly, after the early part of the week has crawled by like the countdown towards a tax audit, it's Thursday. *The* Thursday. At home, I'm edgy all morning. The girls notice nothing, but Elena asks if everything's all right.

'You seem . . .' she begins, but then doesn't know how to finish the sentence. 'I don't know,' she adds, then logs on to her Teams conference.

I have elected not to tell her about the park drama, and I'm not entirely sure why. I feel it would be a strange thing to confess to, unlikely enough for fiction. Or perhaps it's simply nice to have something that takes place *away* from the house and the family unit for a change, and I want to keep it to myself?

I have an early lunch, and then, because I can't wait any longer, I go upstairs to rouse the dog several hours earlier than I normally would. Not expecting me, she is spark out on our bed, the same bed she is forbidden to sleep on. She opens her eyes in surprise, and winds her tongue – which, in its lolling state, is dry like biltong – back into her mouth, and follows me dutifully downstairs.

When was the last time, I wonder, I felt butterflies like this in my stomach?

Elizabeth and Pavlov are already there, Pavlov rocking on his feet.

'I go to the toilet three times already this morning,' he tells us, crows' feet stamped deep into either temple.

Our hellos sound scripted, and feel awkward. No one else is here, and so we walk, for anything better to do. Presently, we find a bench, and sit. Still conversation does not flow. Pavlov keeps looking up, and over towards the gate.

Agatha joins us, similarly agitated. She's left Coco at home, because while it's Olivia that's going to help

157

Lintang find her passport, help her pack her bags and get her out of the house before the wife returns, it's Agatha who is going to drive her away from here, across town in her small electric car, to a refuge she's found that will take her in, look after her, and help her. Agatha has done her research. She found that Lintang fulfilled the criteria for likely trafficking into the country. She is eligible for help. Agatha had sourced the nearest refuge, and it was agreed that this was her best option, at least on a short-term basis. The police did not need to become involved.

'At the very least,' Agatha had told us, 'Lintang will be away, and free of *them*, able to start again somewhere else.'

Pavlov doesn't wear a watch, having once told me that he no longer believed in the concept of time. He wishes he had one now.

'What time is?' he asks.

'It's five minutes after the last time you asked,' Agatha says. 'Just calm down.'

'But where are they?'

'They'll come when they come. Now, let's walk some more.'

The hot sun has bleached the grass yellow. In one corner of the park, the first of the funfair trucks have arrived. The fair is set to open at the end of the month, where it will squat until mid-August. Its presence will disrupt the dog walking circuit and ruin the grass, leaving tracks in the earth that take weeks to grow out. The weekend footballers will have to play elsewhere, or simply postpone their forthcoming fixtures. Consequently, among the walkers, the joggers and the Sunday leaguers, there is a temporary ceasefire: none of them like the funfair. Pavlov calls it an invasion and says that, as a Russian, he would know. The local drug dealers, however, find plenty to celebrate, because wherever young men loiter, there is reliably brisk business. Some of the locals write letters to the council, complaining about the levels of disruption it brings to the surrounding streets. But I'm not sure it brings *any* disruption. People just like to feel put out and inconvenienced, and to have an excuse to write an old-fashioned complaint letter, in pen, on paper.

Dotted around the park right now are sunseekers. On a more normal day, Olivia might be among them, doing her aerobics. Sid arrives, late, on his motor scooter, and announces that his eczema is particularly bad right now.

'Stress,' he says. 'I'm sure of it.'

It ravages the skin on his left cheek and neck, and mottles his thick forearms in a collage of angry pinks and flaky greys. He scratches at it incessantly, and asks for an update on, as he puts it, 'the Lintang situation'.

'Too hot for Rocky to run today,' he says. 'Left him deflated on the kitchen floor.'

Nobody responds to him, and so to help vanquish the silence I find myself telling them that Missy has a rash. When I scratch her in a particular place, I can feel the spots on her flank, and she responds by thumping her back leg like a Disney rabbit. Ordinarily, this is prime dog-walking chat, and would prompt an enthusiastic half-hour discourse at the very least, filled with strenuous advice from Pavlov to avoid taking her to the vet, whom he believes to be an opportunistic and untrustworthy type, but today: nothing. Even Elizabeth stays quiet in silent rumination.

'What time now?' Pavlov says.

'Two fifty.'

'Where is she?!' he says impatiently. 'I need the toilet.'

Agatha offers him a beady eye. 'You should have gone before you left home.'

'I did!'

I find myself thinking how, in just ten minutes' time, all three of the wife's children will not be picked up from school. Each of them will be loitering at the gate, craning their neck, wondering where Lintang is. The school secretary will have to go through the database to find a mobile phone number to call. The wife will be alerted, and the situation will progress from there.

Sid sees them first.

'*There!*'

I look over. It's Olivia, in a hoodie, speedwalking into the park, Lintang rushing to keep up behind her. I try to read their faces, their expressions, desperate for spoilers, and unable to wait to find out in real time what had happened back there, in the house, and why it all took so long, and whether they were successful. I'm desperate to know that everything is still going to – to *plan*. Everyone is.

Olivia looks serious, and, in her hoodie, much too hot. Beside her, Lintang, who is dressed in her familiar stone-washed jeans and her Puffa jacket, is a deathly pale. Her eyes are red-rimmed.

Breathing heavily, panting almost, a spread palm pushed flat against her ribcage to reveal fingernails that, I see now, are chipped and uneven, Olivia begins slowly to grin. She puts her other hand into the kangaroo pouch of her top, retrieves something, then holds it up for inspection. A passport, Lintang's.

'Got it!' she beams.

Beside her, Lintang visibly trembles.

Elizabeth gasps. 'Oh, thank goodness,' she says. 'That's wonderful. *Wonderful!*'

Each of us shuffles slightly forward until we are virtually in a huddle, a rugby scrum waiting for someone to impart tactics.

Olivia bursts into tears. Agatha reaches her first.

Lintang, meanwhile, remains rooted to the spot, a model of contemplative composure. Pavlov asks if she's all right.

'Yes,' she replies.

He offers her a mint, and I feel a curious relief when she accepts.

Fourteen

I am not the one who suggests couples' therapy; Elena is. Ever the pragmatist, she thinks it might be useful for us both to talk through some things. She makes rabbit ears in the air around the words 'some things', which she wouldn't normally do, and so I know it's serious. If I remain outwardly calm-seeming, and I try, then inwardly I panic. We are at the kitchen table when she says it, the dinner things pushed to one side, the wine glasses almost empty, the girls upstairs in their rooms. She says that it's possible we might have lost sight of one another given everything we've gone through these past few years.

Myopically, I ask her what she means, and without

even drawing breath she tells me, counting off each point on the fingers of her left hand, before moving onto her right: my health issues, hers, the perpetual assaults of parenthood alongside the multiple indignities of middle age; the generalised inertia our relationship has so predictably slumped into, how we never talk any more, not really, and how we've become more *housemates* than anything else . . . and other things I'd rather not go into here and now, if that's all right?

When she's quite finished, my ears pop. It's like I'm on an aeroplane that's hit an air pocket and is struggling to relocate its cruising altitude.

'Perhaps,' she suggests quietly, 'talking to someone might help?'

Me feigning a sense of calm is, or was, very much my default setting. I rarely raise my voice, never publicly freak out. I travelled for work with a small group to Australia once, a journey that involved being snowed-in in New York for thirty-six hours, missing the connecting flight in Los Angeles because the photographer had wandered off, and then enduring turbulence the pilot later described to us as his 'worst ever'. The more everyone around me panicked, the more I didn't. One of our group called me 'weirdly Zen', and I took it as a compliment. I don't fear the doctor or the dentist, and I am to a fault painfully reasonable and boringly logical. But if a decade of poor health has taught me anything, it's that my flight or fight reactions are increasingly easily triggered when I detect the threat of genuine danger, and that my amygdala, that small, almond-shaped thing in my brain that scours perpetually for sabre-toothed tigers, is always pulsing a silent siren blare. I've worked hard to quieten it down, but I remain a work in progress.

And so now, while I nod placidly as Elena talks, inside I'm milking the situation for all its dramatic reach, and very necessarily I swiftly create a mind map to help lead me both to, and through, the inevitable next steps. I fast-forward to the separation that will now surely follow, and then the fairly amicable divorce, and tell myself that I shall keep calm, and carry on. I see myself moving out, and into a studio flat, but then immediately scotch this and upgrade to a one-bedroom, to better accommodate the girls when they come to visit on alternate weekends. Will I be able to afford a one-bedroom? I'll have to move away, to the dreary part of the suburbs, more remote, fewer bus routes. It will be a small place, but sufficient, with room enough for my bookcases and my armchair, a sofa bed in the living room, and a small balcony on which I might keep the kind of plants that do well on the balconies of divorced middle-aged men. The flat will be in a neat block set not too far from the high street. It will be on the top floor, as I don't like the sound of footsteps overhead. I hope the lift will be reliable. I'll avoid the misery of other recently divorced types, and avoid too the stain it so often leaves, by keeping myself busy, and by remaining mentally engaged. Of course my life will shrink, but perhaps, I work hard to convince myself, it will also grow more ordered, with less to manage. There is, I tell myself, relief in this. I'll get by.

I imagine that Elena will get custody of the dog, which might just free me up into getting a cat again. I remain a cat person at heart. A vet had once told me that cats were highly adaptable, and that it wasn't cruel to keep one indoors if it had never known a garden. The two of us can adapt together.

Tentatively, I'll make new friends, this despite the fact that I've lately fallen out of the habit. You never forget to ride a bicycle, do you? Divorce is the great leveller, after all, and so finding like-minded souls is hardly a fantasy. People do it all the time. I'll join their ranks. There are evening classes, group activities, weekend men events around campfires. I'll Google them. I know that I won't ever be lonely because I never have been. No one is ever lonely if they read books, and I rarely do anything else. Perhaps I'll become my true self, whatever that is? Either way, I'll gradually rebuild. Life is full of phases, someone once told me. This will simply be another phase. It won't have to be a disaster.

Will it?

'Are you going to say anything, or just sit there?' Elena wonders.

I return to the room, blinking back from my reverie. 'Okay,' I say hastily.

'Okay, *what?*'

'To the therapy,' I say, 'the couples' therapy.'

The fantasy has vanished as quickly as it had arrived. I realise now, less a notion and more a hard, inalienable fact, that I couldn't possibly live without her. Not just because of the upheaval required, but because I love her, irrevocably, unendingly and unambiguously. I always have. We remain very different people, which means we've never been the perfect fit, but that's what I like so much about her. She brings something to me that *I* lack, and I can only hope that I do similar for her. Simply, she is my favourite person. And so if I must now acknowledge that the relationship has been harmed, and that I need to work at it in new and unexpected ways, then I will because I must. There is no conceivable alternative.

'Okay, good,' she says, and reaches her hand across the kitchen table, between the empty wine glasses, to hold mine. Neither of us says anything for what feels like the longest time. The girls walk in. They look at us both in turn, and then at each other. Eyebrows are actively employed.

'What's happened? What's wrong?'

'Who wants dessert?' I say. Their eyes light up, but they remain wary, hedging their enthusiasm in case the offer turns out to be a disappointing reveal, like rice pudding.

'No, no,' I assure them, 'I bought something nice. It's in the fridge.'

In order to retrieve it for them now, I must let go of my wife's hand, and step away.

I sometimes like to imagine the implausible fact of parallel universes – just two of them, I'm not greedy – each running concurrently but increasingly apart from the other. Years ago, I had a choice which to walk into, panicked, and chose poorly. I went somewhere that led to my exposure to a hostile virus that set up home in a body already compromised, and which has been doing its insidious work ever since. What if I hadn't gone? What if I'd said no, and stayed home? Would everything be different?

'When you turn and look back down the years, you glimpse the ghosts of other lives you might have led,' wrote a superior memoirist.

In the parallel universe, perhaps I get to live a life that doesn't require quite so much slowing down quite so early in life. Instead, health prevails and sustains. This other me keeps swimming and cycling and walking, more lengths and ever more miles in that pointless pursuit of Personal Best. In middle age, conscious of landmark birthdays, I take up running, and push my body forwards simply because I always could and still can. Perhaps I spend money on Lycra, and even shave my legs for the aerodynamics of it, who knows? The girls will surely raise their eyes at these self-conscious displays of peak physical fitness in their old man, but I'd enjoy their mockery. In this universe, my marriage doesn't sink into concrete but instead remains buoyant. Bones don't ache, repetition doesn't grate. Bedcovers are thrown off each morning with eagerness, and there are no hospital appointments, no texts from the surgery calling me to successive health checks, no concerned looks from the kindly pharmacist when I go in to pick up yet another prescription. No concerningly high cholesterol levels. No loss of libido, no existential disillusion or distress of living in a world that no longer makes sense as it once did.

This other me doesn't withdraw into myself, nor does he lose sight of the woman he loves.

I have a picture of Elena on my phone that springs into life every time she calls. It's twenty years old, and features her in two dimensions from another, distant life, relaxing on a beach, in a hammock, in Mexico. She is so beautiful here, it's hardly surprising that the phone vibrates. She looks very different now, of course, but not, I realise, in any way diminished. She is radiant, still. She is someone who, in the intervening years, has navigated a career, helped secure mortgages, birthed children, and who has been with me – in the only universe there is for us – through it all, my fierce and loyal ally who thrives on a sustaining selfless kindness. She no doubt has her own parallel universe too, of course, but I married a realist. She remains ever-present.

Late at night, sleepless, I can sometimes convince myself that growing older is nothing but an endurance. But it's also a gift. There's no one I'd rather do it with.

The subject of couples' therapy seems to go away, as many subjects do. It gets mislaid down the sofa, or else somewhere within the habitual melee of everything that is required of us both on any given day, when we are instead looking furiously for the phone charger, or giving the printer one last ultimatum before reaching for a hammer. But then perhaps we don't actually need it, after all? Because it turns out that there is a facilitator already within our midst, whose presence alone will bring us together in ways that we've never quite anticipated. This will come as a pleasant surprise, but then the best surprises are always the most unexpected ones.

For almost fifteen years, our weekends have been arranged around the children's needs. Their social lives are full. But now, they sleep later, and for longer, and when they do manage to come down for breakfast, it's already lunchtime, and they tell us they've made plans for the evening that don't involve us. 'Text you later,' they say as they head for the door, 'bye.'

It's strange to watch them go, but thrilling to witness the fact of their independence. It frees us up, too. No longer required to squeeze the dog walk around their requirements, we suddenly have the novelty of *time*. And so, gradually, and thanks largely to the needs of our small animal, a ritual emerges. We continue to wake up earlier than we need to at the weekend, because habits die hard, have breakfast, and then drive to some nearby woodland where Missy, who can barely believe her luck, leads us through unfamiliar trees dense enough to be viewed by urbanites like us as actual forests, and across trails heavily blanketed by exotic-seeming flora. In the winter, we crunch on frozen ground, and in the summer we seek out cafes that appear to exist as if in a fairytale, carved into the landscape and offering only oat milk options. We wonder at the intricate marvel of the icy spiders' webs that hang like garlanded chandeliers from perimeter fences, and are struck dumb by the beauty of the heron that stands, always alone and unmoving, on a branch, deaf to my pleadings that it launch up into majestic flight. I reach for my phone to catch swans coming heavily in to land on a body of water, and we both hold our breath as a pair of deer just a few feet in front of us (the dog taut on her lead) stoop to lock horns, and then wait to see which of them moves first with all the attention required of chess. On wetter days, we sink into mud, and in the summer watch as the dog leaps from anthill to anthill, her mood close to rapture.

And all the while, the two of us talk. We enjoy for the first time in I don't know how long the simple luxury of a rambling conversation, the kind we used to indulge in back when we were still getting to know one another, and which helped create a bond that would make it possible to endure whatever the future held. Here, we talk about everything of consequence, but also revel in its opposite. We make each other laugh, and recall our years of wanderlust, the countries we visited, and all the trains and boats and planes that took us there. And within all this chatter there is, I think, a tacit awareness between us of relief that both of us still *fit*, and that we actively like one another, even after all this time, despite everything. The love has survived, which itself comes as a pleasant surprise, but the *like* is something that has required attention for some time now.

We discuss the future, impossible to foretell but looming all the same. We decide that we need fresh adventure, in whichever way both of us can manage it now. After years of regimen and routine, and of keeping to a sensible schedule, we crave once more the uncertain and the unknown. We've travelled before, we can do so again. A pipe dream perhaps, and mere fantasy, but I know my wife well. I know that, later, while I sleep, she will be Googling the practicalities of it, and planning ahead for every possibility in the event that we make the dream real.

Throughout our walks, the dog weaves between us both, the umbilical cord that keeps us connected, and each of us comes home wet and muddy and tired, but energised. The impetus behind her earlier suggestion for couples' therapy had been an attempt to bring us back together again. Ultimately, all we really needed was the time and the space, and this was granted to us, eventually, eventually, by the children growing up, and by having a pet that loved to get lost with us.

One of the parks we visit on our longer weekend walks stretches on for 2,500 acres. There are over 600 deer here, red and fallow, horse trails that emit a pungent sawdust whiff, and everywhere underfoot is the squelch of things that take the business of growing and sprouting seriously. There are hills and lakes and, at the weekends, on the roads that bisect it, hundreds of serious-minded cyclists dressed in primary colours who hunch over their bikes and race with kamikaze intent.

During the autumn months, Missy is almost entirely camouflaged amongst these surroundings, fallen leaves attaching themselves to the tendrils of her errant beard where they dangle like basic Christmas decorations, and while Elena and I amble, she chases what she thinks might be squirrels over earth blanketed by colours a thousand shades of brown. One day, the two of us are engaged in conversation about the life/work balance, and the possibilities of an increasingly nomadic lifestyle away from home, via strong wifi, in various cities around the world. We'd live in a succession of Airbnbs and, when not working, would sample the wine and grow fat on the local cheese.

'The dog would come too, of course,' Elena says, and I answer that this is a given, that she is a part of us now.

We turn to register the dog's own thoughts on the subject, to gauge her reaction, but she's not here.

Missy has gone.

Very quickly, we do everything that owners *do* in such a situation. We run at speed in every direction, and we shout, and cry, and curse. We double back on ourselves, and return to the car in case she might be obeying the homing instincts more common with other breeds, and we retrace our steps through the mulch and deeper on into the woods. A dachshund went missing here just last week, killed by deer, or so the rumour mill had it. I suddenly remember a conversation from months ago now – years? – the woman whose Border terrier went missing in the countryside and got stuck down a rabbit hole.

'Look for rabbit holes!' I yell at Elena, now some distance away from me.

Both of us have to Google 'rabbit holes' in order to learn how to spot them, holding our phones high in pursuit of a steady signal. It's late October, every branch of every tree is bare, the ground thick with their discarded leaves. Needles in haystacks would be easier to find.

We grow increasingly exhausted, but still we traipse, calling for a dog who actively likes not always having to pay attention, especially when the alternative for her is to roam wild. There are three million squirrels in the country, and at least half that number have taunted Missy in the last seven years. The chances of her ever catching one are, right now, as likely as us locating the rabbit hole she may be stuck in. It's getting dark.

My amygdala helps to produce snapshots of how the next few days will unfold. A *Missing* poster, a grainy black and white photograph because the printer refuses to do colour, and a plea for her to be found. Red collar, microchipped, answers to the name of 'Missy'. Reward offered, much-loved, much-missed. '*Please call.*'

I recall, too, several of her spent nine lives, a trait she shares with cats. There was the time she disappeared in another wood just after a heavy snowfall that my weather app had failed to predict, the white layering short-wiring her own GPS system. We found her half an hour later up by the car park, icicles in her whiskers, beaming with joy. The time she ran across a frozen lake in pursuit of a ball I'd all too eagerly thrown, and halfway across had fallen through a crack and disappeared beneath the surface. Any requirements for heroism on my part passed mercifully in an instant when she simply clambered back out again, shivered and shook herself, and then elegantly skated back to us with the ball clamped in her mouth, Elena refusing to speak to me for the rest of the day, except to say: 'Don't you ever do that again.' The time one summer afternoon she simply waltzed alone out of the open front door, turned left, then right, up along the main road where she presumably waited at the lights, crossed, and went into the park where she discovered Elizabeth, who called me a moment later – she found my number on the disc that dangles from her collar – and asked me, clearly confused: 'If Missy's here, where are you?'

The sun continues to dip. Texts come from the girls asking about dinner. I look at my watch and see that it's been two hours. We've barely spoken a word to each other, focusing only on the task at hand. We are spare with anguish, but decide that we can't leave, not yet, that we'll wait a little while longer, just in case.

'It's cold,' Elena says. 'Let's go back to the car. We can watch from there.'

Reluctantly, I agree, and we walk slowly back to the now emptied-out car park. As we do so, Missy appears from nowhere and falls into step with us, betraying a total absence of fanfare. She's just trotting along at my heels as if she'd been there all along. The image is so ridiculous that neither of us can believe it. I do a double-take, we both shout, and laugh, then fall to our knees to check whether it really is her, whether she's hurt, or injured, and then we hug her, and both of us are crying, and Missy has no idea why, she's licking the tears from our cheeks, happy and confused, her breath terrible, and then she sits primly and wags her tail, right paw up, requesting a treat, which immediately she is awarded.

At the car, she jumps happily up into it, and lies down across the back seat as if exhausted, something she doesn't usually do. It takes a while for both of us to compose ourselves before the drive home. We keep looking back to make sure she's really there. And she is. Whatever she got up to in those lost couple of hours, she's keeping to herself – for her own memoirs, perhaps.

This deeply unwanted drama serves a secondary purpose, I realise. It brings back unscripted adventure and incident into life, and it brings us together in common purpose. New memories are formed, and both of us become increasingly aware that we never feel more at peace than when walking with her at the weekends, never knowing quite what will happen next, nor where we might end up. What we do know, at least, is that whatever does happen, she will at some point return, will almost certainly eventually return, like the vibratingly magical thing she is.

And besides, I tell myself, obedience is overrated.

Fifteen

Lintang has yet to finish her mint before Olivia disentangles herself from Agatha's embrace, and wipes the tears from her cheeks. She speaks rapidly.

'Quick! The wife. She'll come looking for you.'

She gives Lintang her passport, and watches as she puts it into her backpack. Perhaps for her own benefit as much as Lintang's, Agatha, who assumes control, like relay racers exchanging the baton, tells her again what will happen next. She will drive her across town, and far from here, where a lady at the refuge is expecting her. There, she will be safe. Lintang, who keeps craning her neck to look back over her shoulder, nods and says, 'yes, yes. Yes.'

Elizabeth steps forward. 'We got you this,' she says, pressing into her hand the padded envelope filled with the financial efforts of our fundraising.

Lintang, uncomprehending, receives it, still nodding, her lips thin. Elizabeth hugs her, Olivia hugs her. Me and Pavlov reach out to squeeze her upper arm, a move that seems both rehearsed and paternal, and faintly ridiculous. We wish her good luck, the very best of luck, and watch as she and Agatha now speedwalk in the opposite direction, towards the car. Our gaze lingers, and we watch as they reach the car, get into it, and as Agatha does a slow three-point turn, then drives along the outside perimeter road, before turning left up towards us, to the traffic lights, the main road, and gone. As she passes, I see Lintang sitting upright, staring vacantly ahead, clutching her bag. We all wave, hoping she might wave back. She doesn't.

An emptiness fills in their wake, and it feels almost forlorn. With her departure, Lintang's story has come to an end, at least for all of us. It will be back to dog walking, now.

Elizabeth speaks. 'So what happened, Olivia? Tell us.'

'Of course, yes,' Olivia replies, only too happy to relay their story for us, which she does with an attention to detail only Olivia could muster.

She'd been phlegmatic at first, she explains, the actor preparing for her part: neck stretch, shoulder rolls, diaphragmatic breaths, how now brown cow. Technically, here at number 11 Spring Grove, she was breaking and entering – although Lintang *did* open the door for her, a detail her legal team might wish to bring up in court, if court was where this were headed. Lintang had been standing at the living room window, impatiently awaiting her arrival for several anxious minutes, when at last she saw her coming. It was a little after 1.30 p.m.; the wife had left half an hour previously. The house was theirs.

Olivia smiled through mounting nerves, while Lintang looked ashen. She told Olivia to remove her shoes. 'The lady doesn't allow shoes on the carpet,' she said, closing the door quietly behind her. Olivia took in the wide hallway, and the doors that led through to the living room, the dining room, back towards the kitchen and the garden beyond. There was a staircase that curved elegantly to the right, a chandelier suspended from the high ceiling.

The place was spotless, evidence of Lintang's tireless work in the absolute absence of dust, the fact of nothing out of place. The hallway mirror gleamed, reflecting the image of someone in a hoodie who shouldn't have been there at all.

Lintang led her up the thickly carpeted stairs, two flights to the master bedroom. Arched windows over-looked the silent manicured lawn below, the open velvet curtains standing sentry. The bed's duvet was tight enough to bounce pennies off. She took in the antique chest of drawers, the walk-in wardrobe filled with high-heeled shoes, the recessed light fittings; an entire shelf of handbags. On one bedside table was a folded news-paper and a book on the Second World War, on the other a hairbrush, a bottle of pills, an empty glass. The carpet beneath was deep shag, and hummed with clean-liness. Her feet left soft prints.

To us, Olivia explained how she removed from her

pockets a pair of thin polythene gloves ('fingerprints, DNA'), and encouraged Lintang to relax, and to breathe, as she began to search for the passport. She moved through the walk-in wardrobe, the drawers, the high shelves. On the floor, a safe. Lintang shook her head.

'Not there, I think,' she said.

She led Olivia back downstairs, to the study. 'Maybe here. But it's locked.'

'The key?'

To her surprise, Lintang nodded. 'I found it,' she said, and allowed herself a private smile. She clarified: 'I *think* I found it.'

Together, they descended to the kitchen, radiant from its recent polish. Behind the door of the utility room, Olivia could hear the Pomeranians sniffling and yipping in excited anticipation of the door opening. But this wouldn't be happening any time soon. 2.15 p.m. Lintang opened a cupboard, frowned, then closed it again, before opening another, sighing hard. She brought out a heavy glass jar filled with coins, placed it on the counter, and opened the lid. Rooting around among this mountain of loose and forgotten change, she retrieved a key.

'For the office,' she said. 'It's the spare.'

'You haven't checked?'

Lintang shook her head. 'Not allowed.'

She replaced the jar on its shelf, closed the cupboard door, then reached instinctively for a dust cloth to wipe it clean. She offered Olivia the key, and both went back upstairs. The door was dark oak and solid, the keyhole offering the only glimpse into its hidden world. She tried the key. It fitted. They were in.

Lined with bookshelves that were mostly empty, the centrepiece of the room was a large desk that sat squarely on an ancient-looking, threadbare Turkish rug. Three drawers on either side, a soft leather office chair in between. Olivia pulled at the first drawer, anticipating resistance, but it slid open to reveal pencils, loose change, a button, random staples, elastic bands. Batteries, an old mobile phone, a BlackBerry. Keys and pens, a glasses case.

She tried the other drawers, all of which were open but one. None held anything of particular interest, except the last. In here were letters, still in their open envelopes, bound together with string. There was money, random notes of various denominations and in various currencies. And there were passports: five of them. No, *six*. 2.40 p.m., and the clock on the wall suddenly announcing itself emphatically, its ticking the loudest thing in the room. Lintang asked Olivia to hurry, please to hurry. Olivia flicked through the passports, his, hers, the three children's. And Lintang's.

'We screamed at each other then, I think,' Olivia told us, now bringing Lintang into a hug, the two women smiling broadly in triumph and relief.

The realisation that its retrieval was this easy, that Lintang's incarceration was something she could have broken free from herself months previously, was a factor neither of them acknowledged out loud. But then Lintang's imprisonment had never been completely physical, more a psychological incarceration. Tangible freedom would require much more than mere distance, or the possession of documentation.

'And that's when we made *our escape*!' Olivia said, her

voice leaning into italics. She told how they now went back down to the kitchen where she noticed a small backpack, the kind children take to school. It looked full. She pointed to it as Lintang strapped it tightly across her back.

'Is that it?'

She nodded. 'Yes. My suitcase . . . it is gone.'

It was only after they left and closed the gate behind them, walking briskly towards the park, Olivia said, that the heightened tension of it all hit them both with an adrenaline rush, the bungee rope snapping and yanking them back into the previous freefall. She removed the gloves, and pulled her hood over her head. Any sense of euphoria she'd anticipated was now manifesting instead into a great blossoming panic. Beside her, Lintang was still a deathly pale, shuffling as if she'd lost the power to walk, both of them clearly desperate now to flee, and to leave the house far behind.

But then: the *wife*.

Suddenly, she was there, on the street, walking towards them. One moment there was an empty stretch of pavement, the next there was *her*. Olivia was now required to go off script. She'd never actually seen the wife before, but knew in an instant – 'in my very bones,' she said later – that this was her. Gazing into her phone, her hair salon-fresh and catching the light to create a misleading halo. Beside Olivia, Lintang froze, and the air around them seemed to warp, like on airport runways.

'Quick,' Olivia said, and bustled Lintang into the road,

telling her to crouch down behind a parked car. 'Don't move.'

Olivia returned to the pavement, pulled down her hood, shook out her hair, and walked on. The wife, she saw, was wearing expensive shoes which clacked like Morse code. The gap between them closed. She looked up now, but paid little attention to the young woman striding towards her. They crossed paths and their eyes met, Olivia affording her a beaming smile that seemed momentarily to confuse her.

'Lovely day!' she announced loudly, and the wife frowned, and clacked on. Olivia slowed, listened to the gate somewhere behind her swing open and then shut, the expensive shoes climbing the steps to number 11, and disappearing into the house. She turned, ran out into the road, saw Lintang still crouching, passive as a tortoise, and urged her to run towards her. They linked hands, crossed over the road and into the park, 'where all of you were waiting for us.'

Olivia appears visibly at this point to deflate.

'I don't know about you,' she says, 'but I need a stiff drink.'

But now there is a woman, approaching fast. The wife, again.

She is familiar to each of us, though not by sight, and I'm only aware of who it is when I see Olivia freeze. She comes bustling over.

'Excuse me!' she says. Her voice is loud and shrill, and carries on the warm air like musical notes. Her hair really does look expensive. 'Have you seen my cleaner?' she asks.

'Your *cleaner*?' Pavlov says.

She casts wildly around the park, clutching at her bare upper arms with her hands. 'Lintang,' she clarifies with a palpable impatience. 'She works for me, for our family. She comes here with the dogs, Pomeranians, three of them. You must know them.'

Pavlov shrugs. 'I do not see any Pomeranians here, do you?'

'No, *no*.' The impatience is greater now. 'The dogs are at home,' she says, 'but—'

'And so maybe she is home, too, this *cleaner* of yours?' Pavlov, having been sidelined for so much of this, is enjoying himself.

The wife takes a slow, deep breath, as if measuring her response by vowel and consonant. She says that if Lintang were home, she wouldn't be here looking for her now, would she? She describes Lintang to us, using hands to denote height. 'I thought,' she says, 'that you might have seen her here sometimes? With your dogs?'

'No,' Pavlov says.

There is safety in numbers, of course, which is probably why we feel quite so confident in facing her, and in facing her down. There is much we could say, and much we might want to say, but action has said it all, already. The wife looks confused, angry. From this, I know each of us derives satisfaction.

'Perhaps,' Olivia offers, 'she's at another park?'

The wife looks at Olivia now for a moment too long, as if trying to place her.

'No,' she says. 'She's not allowed at other parks, only this one—'

'Not *allowed*?' Pavlov says.

But the wife has had enough of this, and of us, and is already moving on in search of other people to whom she can pose the same question. She is brisk and irritated. Panic must surely be descending amidst the realisation of what might have happened here – no, of what has *surely* happened here: that Lintang has gone.

Pavlov points. 'Look,' he says, beginning to laugh. 'She's approaching Benji. This should be fun.'

In the distance, we watch as she talks to Benji. When Tupac saunters over, betraying an immediate interest in her and her unfamiliar scent, she stumbles backwards and almost falls, then brings both hands up to her mouth as if to stifle a scream.

Back at home, life unfolds as usual. There are unopened letters on the table, and someone has left the bedroom light on. The framed photograph in the hallway that claims, in neon, EVERYTHING IS GOING TO BE ALL RIGHT, sits skewed at an angle, knocked there by a careless elbow on the way up the stairs.

The girls ask why I was such a long time, and why I didn't come home with shopping, with food, but they don't seem much interested in an answer. Upstairs, Elena is on a conference call that will extend into, and well beyond, dinnertime. In the kitchen, I turn on the television to a daily teatime quiz show. I mean to feed Missy, but forget and boil water for the girls' pasta instead, and then stand watching the TV screen, locating the remote control to turn the sound up higher. I answer correctly eight questions in the cash builder round, which is four more than the contestant manages, and I turn around to see if the girls are impressed, but they're watching their phones. The dog kicks at her empty bowl, sending it skittering across the floor, secure in the knowledge that I will eventually take the hint.

Over the weeks that follow, the afternoon walks revert so comprehensively back to normal, and without incident, that even Elena notices.

'You're home early,' she says one day.

'Early?'

'Well, your walks have been getting longer and longer recently . . .'

I shrug my shoulders.

'Are you all right? You seem, I don't know, a little flat lately.'

When I tell her what had been occupying me these past few months, all the way up to its unlikely denouement and my own admittedly minimal involvement in it, she appraises me coolly, and with widening eyes. This deep into our relationship, and I can surprise her still. 'Really?' she says, and initially I wonder whether she believes me, comparing once more her dog walking experiences with mine, and measuring the discrepancy between them. But she's happy for me, I think, happy that I'd had this outlet, that I'd been invited into an unforeseen new world.

But it's true that I feel a certain deflation following the events of that Thursday afternoon. Relief, too, of course, because Lintang is free, but her absence has undone the group somewhat. Small talk no longer seems to quite suffice, and I'm aware that the momentum and purpose that had been built into my days has now vanished. It takes me a while to accept that life simply slots back into its everyday inaction, as if it had been waiting for me all along. Olivia is no longer a daily presence at the park, and in fact I see her less and less over the coming weeks, and then never again, at least not in the flesh. Three years later, I'm watching a police procedural on Sunday night television, and there she is, Olivia, on screen. She was right: the camera really does love her. She's playing a young detective sergeant who goes undercover on an oil rig somewhere in the North Sea. In the fourth episode of six, she is required to rabbit punch an assailant, felling him instantly. I see the look of satisfaction in the detective sergeant's face, and I recall a similar look she'd given me years previously, holding that passport up in her hand and shaking it as if to put out a flame.

'I used to know her,' I say.

Elizabeth is also absent. After a week, Pavlov begins to worry. When she does at last return, I find that she looks every one of her eight decades. Betty, she tells me, had been ill, sleepless nights and medication, lots of care and attention.

'But she's better now, I think,' she says, as if to reassure herself.

I had noticed that her dog had lost weight recently,

but in that slow, incremental way of the apocryphal frog in the boiling water, I also didn't, not really. I simply reconfigured the image of her in my mind to match the one in front of my face. It's a belated realisation, then, that I see she *is* incrementally wasting away.

'The vet,' Elizabeth continues, 'says that because of her age – she's twelve now – because of her age she won't be doing quite so much running on ahead of me. But that's okay, I like her by my side.' She nods, and offers a rigid smile that betrays the saddest eyes.

The letter, clutched by an excited Agatha, arrives in late August. The funfair has gone, but its track marks remain. We walk together across yellow, grooved grass.

'News from Lintang!' Agatha says. 'She's fine, she's good.'

Hello Agatha,

I hope you are well. I am writing to let you know that I am well. It is good here in the refuge, there are many people like me, though none from my country, but no matter, it's okay. The people are friendly and they are helping me with my visa application form, and they say they are confident I will get something which is called I think Permission to Remain. When I get this I will be able to work, perhaps as a cleaner again but through an agency that is called Ethical. I will then be able to get my own place, and to start sending money home.

I have spoken to my family! They are well, my girls are

good, I think. I told them the truth what has happened to me, and they are very sorry.

I also tell them about you all, and how kind you have been to me. When I came here I meet only bad people, so my heart is full that I got to meet some good people too. All of you helped me, and I wish to say that I am very grateful, and that I won't forget you. And please can you say thank you to Olivia for helping me with my passport that day. She has a fierce spirit!

Thank you again, sayangku.
Your friend,
Lintang

The Pomeranians have disappeared from the park too, leaving me to ponder their fate. On some days, as the summer fades and autumn begins to confetti the earth, I find myself again walking up Spring Grove on the long way home. It continues to draw my curiosity. The house remains its implacable self. Whatever secrets it contains within it, it keeps its counsel. The gate stays shut.

And so the long-running daily event I'd been hooked on has come to its inevitable conclusion, replete with its unlikely hopeful ending.

What now?

Sixteen

For several weeks, I don't see Elizabeth at all. The park feels curiously empty without her in it, the quiet maternal presence she exuded, the stealthy life force of her. Despite her age, her twice-daily walks occurred here like clockwork for a dozen years. She'd become close to many people, someone whose conversational versatility meant that she could connect with whomever she was speaking to, moulding herself to their own respective shapes. In Pavlov's company, she was obligingly passive, allowing him the centre stage he required, but away from it she could talk uninterrupted about her own life, her widowhood, the benefits of a positive mindset, the reviving power of Pilates, and the daughters and grandchildren she cared for so much. I never heard an unkind word from her, and never saw her betray anything but fondness for all. Allowing Pavlov an open window for his unreconstructed maleness was an ongoing kindness. She put up with him, indulged him, and perhaps, in her own way, loved him a little bit, too.

It was towards Pavlov that I once saw her commit an act of boundless generosity I don't think I'll ever forget. It had taken place the previous Christmas. At home, I had had a long, lingering lunch with Elena and the girls, the food too much and too rich, the heating set too high, and so, craving the cold slap of some fresh air, I took the dog to the park while the girls wrestled with Monopoly. Today was the day for family and the determined abnegation of habitual duty, and so the park was almost entirely empty. But Pavlov was here, of course, Dog hopping reliably alongside. I thought they looked a little lost in their solitude, cast out and superfluous, this despite his repeated insistence that solitude was his preferred state.

Nevertheless, he brightened visibly when he looked up to see Missy running over, with me in slower pursuit. He jokingly berated me for abandoning kin on a day like this, but then promptly shook my hand. Pavlov had never shaken my hand before.

'You are doing this not just for the dog, I think,' he chuckled.

I'd always believed Christmas to be a hard time for him, his mother long dead, an older sister he rarely saw, the few remaining friendships having fizzled out years previously. I never questioned him on it, though. There are some things we must keep to ourselves.

'Is nice to see you, of course, but I like park like this,' he said, and then, to clarify: 'Empty.'

I asked whether he was having a nice day, and he scoffed.

'I do not like such traditions, do not trust them. I am not religious. Is relief, I tell you, not to have to buy presents for anyone any more. But, hey, happy Christmas to you all the same! Did you eat well?'

Not waiting for an answer, he continued. 'Myself and Dog, we have microwave meal from Co-op waiting for us in the fridge.' He grinned broadly, feigning an appetite duly whetted.

We began our circuit, and before long it was just another day, and perhaps all the more reassuring for it. Missy turned, and went dashing off in pursuit of a private intent, and as I watched her go saw Elizabeth and Betty arriving. In Elizabeth's hand was a bulging carrier bag. Missy bounded around her with greater excitement than usual. Behind Elizabeth followed a young woman with precisely the same features, later revealed as her daughter, here for a week from Australia. Introductions were made, and as we said our hellos I watched the daughter look over at Pavlov with interest, and perhaps the slightest judgement. Elizabeth explained that her grandchildren were back at her house with her son-in-law. They'd all caught a cold on the flight over, and now Elizabeth was struggling with one too, typically without complaint.

'And so why are you here!' Pavlov boomed.

By now, the dogs were all over her, biting at the unusually fragrant air that surrounded her, tongues lolling.

'Here,' she said to Pavlov, lifting the carrier bag towards him.

'What is this?' he asked.

'It's for you,' she said, 'for Christmas. A bit of lunch. I know you don't go in for these things, but—'

Her daughter interrupted. 'It's turkey, roast potatoes, and all the trimmings. Mum put some aside for you specially, and insisted we come and bring it to you.'

'I knew you'd be here, you see,' Elizabeth told him.

Pavlov looked from daughter to mother, his eyes shining bright.

'Anyway,' Elizabeth said, 'must get back, the children are expecting us. Happy Christmas to both of you. And eat well, Pavlov.'

Pavlov swallowed hard, and called out a clarion 'thank you, thank you!' to her. She turned and smiled, and then her daughter slipped an arm into hers, and off they walked back across the damp grass, towards home.

After three weeks, I see her one afternoon, Elizabeth. She's walking sturdily around the park's path on her own, her head down, dressed in a rain jacket, blue trousers that finish at the ankle, and sensible walking shoes. She's at the furthest distance she can be within these gates, but Missy's sixth sense is as acute as her eyesight, and off she hares. When she reaches her, she jumps up, deliriously happy and knowingly expectant. Elizabeth, who has cataracts and cannot see very far at all, looks blindly up for me before retrieving from her pocket a treat. I wave elaborately, air traffic control coaxing a passenger jet safely to its gate, and only when I fear that this could go on for rather too long do I break out into a gentle jog. When eventually she sees me, she waves.

'Elizabeth! How are you?'

She nods.

'Where's Betty?' I say.

The howl that escapes her mouth contains decibels, and her tears fall with almost projectile force as she hides her face behind her hands.

'I'm sorry,' she says after a moment, 'but Betty, she died. She died twenty-two days ago.'

This is my first canine death. I stammer for words, find none worthy, and in return simply sympathise. I sound like an American TV cop when I tell her that I'm sorry for her loss.

She continues to cry while explaining that, after rallying, Betty had become ill again. She refused to walk, then refused all food. After a series of investigations, the vet diagnosed cancer of the kidneys which had spread to her spine.

'They told me she was in pain, and that she'd been bearing it because, well, because dogs do.'

She shakes with grief.

'And I never knew, because she never told me. She didn't tell me she was in pain, unless of course she did, and I just didn't pay any notice, because I didn't want to, because I was too afraid of losing her . . .'

She falls forward now into my arms, and I catch her, staggering back.

'They gave me painkillers to give her over a couple

of days, and then told me to bring her in after the weekend. I had a final Sunday with her in the house. And then I took her in on Monday, and that's when they, when they . . .

'I couldn't get out of bed after that,' she says, 'couldn't leave the house, not for weeks.'

She tells me that her doctor always reminds her of the importance of exercising daily, for her bones, her joints, but that she couldn't face coming back here, not at first.

'It was Pavlov who made me. He came to my house one day. I didn't even know he knew my address. He came to the house, knocked on the door, and invited himself in, sitting at my kitchen table. It was so strange, his presence, there in my kitchen, and not at the park where I'm used to him being. All the years I've known him, I never invited him for tea. When I asked how he knew where I lived, he said that he had friends in the KGB. A joke, I think. I laughed. He told me he guessed that something must have happened to Betty, and, oh, he was lovely, Nick, just lovely, such a comfort to me. I told him I was too old to get another dog, and how broken-hearted I was without one, but he explained that he, and that all of you in fact, that you'd share your dogs *with* me, and that I should just come back to the park, same as before, every morning and afternoon, just to walk, because the dogs would come flocking to me, because, he said, because the dogs loved me, they all loved me.'

She looks down at Missy now with grateful, damp eyes.

'And *she* has!' she says, bending to stroke her. 'I thought it would be too painful, and to be honest with you, it is, it's horrible, but it's also lovely. I saw Agatha and Coco earlier, and they were so sweet, and now you. It's lovely that Missy hasn't forgotten me, but I still just miss her so much, you know? Betty. I miss Betty so very much.'

Guided more by her appetite than by any instinctive reading of the situation, Missy now stands up on her hind legs and places her two front paws on Elizabeth's thighs. Elizabeth deliberately mistakes it for affection, because people do, and she showers the dog with fuss and attention, the elderly woman and the middle-aged dog connected by a shared fondness, and friendship, and by the offering of something to chew on.

'You're a darling girl,' she tells her, squeezing Missy's otter face between papery hands, 'a darling girl.'

Much like life, dog walking for me changes over the years. The older my animal gets, the less interest she sparks in others. It happens, it's universal. The world favours youth, even here. As a puppy, she'd been a social magnet, and drew people towards her. But at age seven, forty-nine in human years, even though still trim and handsome, not much grey yet, she's nevertheless easier to overlook, her earlier cachet gone, like the pop star whose fifteen minutes have elapsed. This doesn't trouble her at all, because correspondingly she has lost all interest in other dogs too, and those that do dare approach her are likely to get short shrift. She also loses interest in people, and aside from those she already knows and holds in affection, no longer has the attention span, or patience, for anyone new. (In this, we have much in common.) In the early days, we'd been one another's social experiment; now we are simply part of the local landscape, another bloke, another mutt.

She's also more likely to get me into trouble these days, her ongoing irascibility igniting within her a wilful unpredictability.

'You want to control your dog,' a woman tells me one day after Missy snaps at a six-month-old schnauzer. 'Put a muzzle on her, at least, or keep her on the lead. Because I swear,' she adds, 'it's people like you who . . .'

And so on.

Though these are intermittent incidents only, they serve to put me on perpetual alert. One week, when Elena is away for work, I am required to take the morning shift. The grass is heavy with its dew, the streets beyond it gridlocked with oversized cars containing children late for school. I watch as two people arrive in the park. They could be anywhere between their mid-thirties and late-fifties, both of them dressed in the stained leisure-wear gear that suggests they might, on occasion, sleep rough. They find a bench, and sit. The woman places a plastic bag on the space between them, from which she draws out two brown bottles of stout, a single can of Special Brew, a packet of cigarettes and a lighter, and lines up each neatly alongside the other. This sense of ritual hypnotises us, and we watch like it's a spectator sport. She retrieves some baby wipes from the bag, and proceeds to clean her face, her exposed arms. The man lights two cigarettes, and passes one to her. Now she removes an aerosol deodorant, which she sprays onto her neck, and along both legs of her sweatpants. He opens one of the bottles of stout, which they share. Last from the bag come two sausage rolls. He places them on his lap, and I wish he hadn't because it is this that prompts Missy to approach. I try to restrain her by grabbing her, but she's too quick. The correct behaviour now would be to go after her, to hook my fingers into her collar and drag her back. Instead, I stay where I am, and hope passively that – what? – that the situation will resolve itself amenably while I watch meekly on, a pitiful lack of action that I fear sums up so much about my entire approach to life.

It takes them a moment to notice her. When they do, they appraise her coolly and not, I think, with fondness. They might not be dog lovers.

'What's his name?'

I tell them.

The man frowns. 'Strange name for a boy. Does he bite?'

Missy, in front of him now, does her hind leg trick thing again, her two front paws coming slowly to settle on the man's knees, leaving wet prints.

'Go on,' he tells her, 'fuck off.'

Disappointingly, she doesn't, and so he brushes her forcefully off. She bounces back up again, aware, or so she thinks, of the game here, and eager to play in ultimate pursuit of inevitable reward.

The man looks up at me now from underneath a pair of eyebrows turned suddenly malevolent.

'If you don't control your dog, I'll control him for you,' he says.

What happens next takes a moment, just a moment. Perhaps less. For an older dog, she's quick. During the time that extends between *his* warning and *my* calling the dog back to heel, she makes her move. Not once, but twice. *That* quick. I don't register what I'm seeing in real time because my brain doesn't work that fast, but I do come to comprehend it a second later, like on a film, or an action replay. She grabs one sausage roll, and then the other, securing both between her teeth, then springs back to the ground, pivots and runs with the kind of momentum she only very rarely employs these days. She's an arrow, a dart, a speeding train – *gone*.

The man erupts. He's on his feet, shouting and swearing, mouth open wide. He's angry, livid, incandescent. The bottle of stout tumbles to the ground, and a ribbon of its contents splashes up onto the woman's perfumed sweatpants.

'*Oi!*' she shouts.

There is of course a code of conduct here, and the right thing to do. But I'm afraid that my instincts betray me, fight or flight, and so I do as the dog had done. I turn and run. I run, both *away* from them and in pursuit of *her*. Fear makes me fast.

There are times I wish I had never got the stupid dog in the first place, and had simply tried again with gerbils, or perhaps a placid cat. The older she gets, the more the levels of liability continue to rise. At home she remains mostly a balm, a sunny delight, but as the girls grow and make the joyful discovery that Uber delivers food, transforming their bedrooms into an illicit temptation for her as they come to reek of days' old pizza slices and fries, she becomes scavenger, entering their rooms most days after they've left for school. If there's any food in there anywhere, in the bins, beneath the duvet, a medium-high shelf, she'll find it. This causes ketchup and grease stains, and soils clothes that had been strewn innocently across the floor, and the girls blame the dog, and I blame the girls, and the argument, which is maddeningly circular, goes around and around and around. We get locks for the doors.

One afternoon, she finds an unsmoked spliff on the pavement by the bus stop, and elects to eat it. The whites of her eyes grow bloodshot with paranoia, and she spends the remainder of the day listing a little to the left.

I take to walking her on an extendable lead, and my trigger finger that flicks the switch to stop her from suddenly straying, or attacking people, develops strain pain. Meanwhile, she grows weary of having to return to the same old green space day after day. Perhaps dogs, too, have boredom thresholds, because when we leave the house now and I customarily turn left at the garden gate, she refuses to follow and will only concede at all on the promise of treats being dispensed at timely inter-vals. Once in the park itself, it takes a while to fall into our usual rhythm, and when it's time to leave she proves similarly recalcitrant, as if now that she is here, we may as well remain. Stubbornly she sits, happy to test just how extendable the lead really is, forcing passers-by to step over it, their dogs under.

One afternoon, she insists we go in another direction entirely, and while I think that she wants us to head back to the less-visited park further down the road, she has other ideas, pulling me between parked cars and through the heavy gate that leads into the graveyard. This is used in the mornings and afternoons by young families as a shortcut between the estate and the school, and frequented after dark by dealers to sell their product; it otherwise appears to be appealingly uninhabited. Very quickly she comes to love it here, and so do I. It becomes our regular haunt.

Much of it boasts graves over a hundred years old, some partially collapsed in on themselves, their headstones sunk into the soft earth. Here are soldiers, babies and unaccountably old women who lived to a ripe age through both world wars. Several have joined 'God in his heaven', others have 'fallen asleep in Jesus'. One bears nothing but a single name: CRISPIN, another reads RIP CROUCHERS. Blackberries grow by the thousand in the summer, and we see cats, and rabbits, the occasional fox. Everything is overgrown, blissfully calm and slightly sinister. Hitchcockian crows gather in the late afternoon, where they monitor us with beady interest from their perches, so clearly talking about us as we cower beneath them. Every now and then, I see tiny mice running between the graves. The cats that loiter nearby, I know, are mostly here for them. With the exception of the occasional mourner, whom we always avoid to allow them their vigils uninterrupted, we are alone. It suits us both. Like the rest of the world, I've succumbed to AirPods, and so in place of exchanges with strangers, I now just listen to podcasts, thousands of curated conversations with people who possess even more opinions than

Pavlov. At my feet, the dog runs and runs, endlessly assailed by the innumerable smells unleashed by the gradually erupting undergrowth that strives towards the sky to reveal its mysterious riches. There is nowhere she would rather be.

It does sometimes strike me that, in stalking these shrouded paths and alleyways day after day, we are mostly all alone here, except that we're not, not at all. We have each other.

From time to time, I do manage to tempt her back to the usual place, and when I do, Pavlov is reliably present. But not Elizabeth, not any more. Pavlov tells me that she is ailing now, and needs to walk less, and to rest.

'But she is fine, my friend. She will outlive us all,' he says, a great tenderness to his white lie.

Pavlov himself is struggling. He's beginning to look tired in a way that has little to do with lack of sleep, and his conversational prowess, now without the restorative presence of Elizabeth, has turned dour.

'I'm reading Dostoevsky again,' he says. 'Is bleak, you know? I like it.'

We see Agatha occasionally, and one afternoon she tells us that she's heard again from Lintang. She is now settled in a new job with an ethical cleaning company, but no longer works as a cleaner herself. Instead, she's helping newcomers to the industry to settle, establish themselves here, to be aware of their rights and assert them. She has set up a union to help improve standards for immigrant domestic workers.

'It takes up all her time, I think, but she seems to be happy,' Agatha says. 'Also, she's pregnant. I don't know the details.'

'By who?' Pavlov asks.

'I don't know, I just told you that.'

'By *whom*,' I say, and immediately wish I hadn't.

I notice increasingly that there are different people now in the park, younger couples with youthful dogs. The new breed, in both senses. It seems that everyone has a puppy now, a consequence of all that working from home perhaps, and these they fret over with an attention and hypervigilance that, to Pavlov at least, is proof that none have ever had dogs before, and still don't know quite how to behave around them. He calls them snowflakes. They congregate every afternoon after the school pick-up, each of them alert with caution, refusing to let their charges off the lead, but always cooing appreciatively at their antics, and taking endless photographs of them. Missy, like Pavlov, won't go anywhere near them.

Pavlov sits more and walks less, an increasingly grizzled Dog at his feet, grey muzzle flat on the ground in front of him, fully snoring even while wide awake. When we do meet, we keep the conversation to books, TV, music. He has soon read the entire Dostoevsky canon, and is now reading Proust.

It's on one of these increasingly rare afternoons together that we again spot Keith, along with his Alsatian and cockatoo, parading past, each resplendent in their signature white. I haven't seen them for many months, and in fact had forgotten all about them. I point him out to Pavlov, who nods disinterestedly, Keith another male in this particular savanna he has failed to fully bond with.

As they approach our bench, I raise my hand in greeting, but Keith as ever walks blithely past, implacable, unresponsive, coolly aloof. In his wake, Pavlov turns to look at me, his expression withering.

'You do know he's blind?' he says.

'Keith?' I say, redundantly. The revelation stuns me.

'Of course! Why do you think he wears those sunglasses, always keep to the path? Why is his dog always leading him?'

I look over at them with a new awareness. The dog is on a regular lead, not the harness I might have expected, but I do notice now, for the first time, a certain manner to Keith's walk, a suggestion of formality and studied concentration.

I shrug my shoulders. 'I didn't know,' I say. 'I suppose I never thought about it.'

'For a writer, Nick,' Pavlov says, 'you don't notice much, do you?'

A few months later, Dog dies too. The park is gradually filling up with ghosts. I don't witness Pavlov's distress because he stays deliberately away. It's Agatha who tells me, and I wonder how she knows.

'He's doing okay,' she says, 'but it's hit him hard, I think.'

I want to reach out, but know that I can't. I don't know where he lives, I don't have his number. Probably he wouldn't welcome the intrusion anyway, the crossing of boundaries he himself so rarely crosses. Our only means of communication has been in this park, in person. I know that Pavlov is a stoic, and so in much the same way he has learned to walk through his pain, he will surely bear this loss, too. I fervently hope this to be true.

One afternoon, I'm cycling to the shops shortly after lunch. It's a bright, cold day, the streets full of shoppers. I notice a familiar face, Pavlov's. He is outside the super-market, laden with two shopping bags, and looks at once exactly the same but also entirely different. It's a shock to see him so far from his natural habitat, and I hesitate for only a second before calling out.

He looks up. He looks tired.

'My friend,' he says. 'Did not recognise you without the dog. Also, I never seen you on a bicycle before. It suits you!'

He places both carrier bags on the pavement, the tins and frozen goods within making the plastic distend and swell, and he tells me what happened, how, several weeks ago now, he woke up to Dog at the end of his bed, rigid, already cold to the touch.

'Dead many hours,' he says, his voice trembling. He holds up a silencing hand. 'Please,' he tells me, 'say nothing.'

I put my hand on his shoulder. 'I'm so sorry,' I say, 'I'm just so sorry.'

'Is okay,' he answers. 'Is life. And what is life, you know? Is a series of challenges for which we must find a solution. Losing Dog is just my latest challenge.' He shrugs. 'I'm still looking for this solution.'

'Can I buy you a coffee?'

He shakes his head. 'Thank you, but no. Listen,' he says, 'make the most of everything you got, you understand me? Make most of it. Be aware. Be mindful – like all those meditation idiots tell us all the time. Don't let things pass you by while you are looking somewhere else, not paying attention. Enjoy family, your wife, the girls. Missy. Life, it goes on, you know? Day after day, everything the same, yes, but it passes, it passes so quick, and when it does and you realise this, then you're lost. So find the positive in every day, even if, like Benji, it just means trying to find where you left your shoes. Okay?'

Shoppers continue to stream around us, our presence interrupting their flow. Aware that this patch of pavement might not be the best place for Pavlov's existentialism, I ask again whether I might buy him a coffee, and point to the cafe a few feet from where we're standing. 'Cake too, if you like? Anything you want.'

He ignores the question. 'You know,' he says, 'I have lots of things to say to you that are deep and profound, like philosopher, but I have frozen things in here,' he points to the shopping bags at his feet, 'that have to go into freezer, and fresh things also for the fridge, some fruit, vegetables. Since Dog died, I'm trying to live more healthy. No more tins for me!'

We both glance down at the shopping bags, in which the baked beans are singularly failing to conceal themselves.

'Okay, okay,' he laughs, '*some* tins, but less than before, yes? Anyway, no time for deep and profound conversation, not today. I'm sorry, my friend, but I will see you soon. Live your life, Nick,' he says. 'Live your life well.'

I watch him as he stoops to pick up the bags, and flinches at the strain involved.

'Now go,' he says.

It's a high summer's day, Sunday. Everyone in the street is out in their gardens. One neighbour starts up his chainsaw, which he does most mornings during August from eight o'clock, to begin the laborious process of cutting long strips of wood into small chunks for no reason other than the satisfaction of creating something compact and manageable from something large and unwieldy. He's seventy-two years old, and lives with his ninety-five-year-old mother. Both are in different stages of Alzheimer's; at Christmas, he posts through my door a hand-delivered card made out to 'Mike', and a few days later posts another one. A sweet, gentle man, he's a former carpenter now lost mostly within the caverns of his own mind. Sawing wood provides him with a focus, a pleasing muscle memory he is still able to perform without thought, but whose noise splits the air in two.

Elena frowns. 'Shall we go to the river?'

Missy has not grown any more accustomed to the heat in her advancing years. She's ever more set in her ways, ever more peculiar in her particular habits. Dazed and sunstruck in the sunshine, she nevertheless insists on lying on the paving stones until she sizzles so much you could fry an egg on her. I have to physically shift her into the shade, where she pants heavily and visibly deflates, like a tyre with a puncture. Her only respite is water, and so we tend to make trips on days like this to a small bend in the river a fifteen-minute drive away, where people swim and sunbathe, and congregate over picnics and raging barbecue fires. Here, the water is brown and murky for all the reasons we have come to learn about our rivers these last few years, but she, like everyone else, still swims in it all the same. Once refreshed, she seeks out a stick for me to throw, and for her to fetch. She's not interested in tennis balls any more.

And so her decision, right now, to suddenly pursue a tennis ball that has been thrown high into the air before landing with a satisfying plop at some considerable distance from the shoreline is at first confusing, and then concerning. It was thrown by the owner of a Labrador, but the Labrador didn't see the ball, didn't track it, didn't watch it land, doesn't care.

Missy paddles into the middle of the river. Her jaw is open, and she swallows great gulps of water. When she reaches the ball, she attempts to bite down on it, but the ball is big, her jaw's reach smaller than that of a Labrador. Her efforts simply propel the ball further and further away, which requires her to repeat her attempt time and again, which merely pushes the ball further still downriver and out of sight. If you could define madness in one single pointless pursuit, this is it. Stupid, stupid dog. I call her back because instinct tells me to, irrespective of the certainty that she'll pay no attention.

She pays no attention.

The occasional surfboarder and canoeist pass her. Further downriver, a cruiser looms threateningly into view.

The girls begin to shout, their pitch rising to a scream,

the dog's name repeated over and over again. 'Do something!' they tell me, but I'm helpless – she is too far for any of us to swim to, and none of us is a particularly strong swimmer anyway. Elena pleads with her to come back, and does that clicking thing with her tongue she's always convinced the dog responds to. She doesn't. She is swallowing more water, and sometimes she goes under, a brown dog disappearing into brown murk, the tennis ball continuing to elude capture. At the shoreline, an audience has gathered. A woman joins us, the Labrador's owner.

'That's my ball,' she says.

It's Elena who takes definitive action. The cruiser is getting closer all the time, bearing down. 'Help!' Elena says to a passing kayaker. Then louder: '*Help!*'

The audience chatter increases. 'He's going to drown,' I hear someone say.

She.

Three kayakers ignore her, but the fourth doesn't. A rotund man crammed into the circular seating space, he changes direction, paddles faster and angles his body forward. When at last he's alongside, he grabs her by the scruff of the neck, lifts her free of the water, and drops her onto his lap. There are cheers and applause, followed immediately by laughter as Missy shakes her coat dry, drenching him thoroughly. I watch as he turns to see the cruiser now perilously close, but he doesn't panic, he simply paddles with determined forward motion towards the shore. Beside me, the girls whimper in relief. When he's within touching distance, Missy suddenly jumps from his lap back into the water, and we send out a volley of gratitude to the man, who merely nods with the effortless nonchalance of one who does this sort of thing all the time. But then each of us watches horrified as the dog, the stupid, stupid dog, turns sharply and begins to doggy-paddle her way back out towards the middle of the river, where the ball still bobs, now in the cruiser's wake. A collective howl of laughter erupts, cruel jeers too. We are providing the day's entertainment here. I resolve that if anyone *does* manage to save her from drowning today and delivers her safely back to shore, then I will surely kill her myself.

The kayaker, my hero, is unfazed, and simply resumes operations. He knows what he's doing now. He reaches her, grabs her again by the scruff of the neck, but now tightly clasps her between his legs while paddling back with only one arm in order to keep her firmly in place with the other. I wade out to meet him, up to the thighs, and the exchange is successfully made. Later, I will learn that my water-resistant watch isn't water resistant, and that my trainers, suede, are ruined. The girls huddle around the drenched dog, who promptly vomits up at least a pint of water. They cuddle her, and tell her off. She wags her tail.

'I'm sorry,' says the Labrador owner, 'but that's still my ball out there. What are you going to do about it?'

Hours later, back at home, and after bringing up several more pints of river water, she curls up on her bed in the kitchen, as exhausted as I've ever seen her.

'We are *never* taking her back there again,' the girls say, themselves spent by the drama. I counter this by reminding them, and myself, that this is simply what dogs *do*. They lead us astray, add incident to our lives, and provide surprising narrative arcs to otherwise lazy summer days.

She looks up at each of us in turn, as if she knows she's being spoken about. She tilts her head, just in case it helps.

I don't take her out again for hours, until the sun has begun its slow descent. The sky is cloudless, electric blue still, but now with added distant contrails painting its canvas in pink and purple streaks before dissolving into smouldering grey ash. It's cooler at last, the paving stones deep in shadow. The streets are deserted, everyone at home in front of the television, its pulsing light flashing from a succession of living room windows as I pass them, front doors flung open in the hope of catching a breeze. The park is empty, too. Missy, who seems to have recovered from the morning's incident in the way that dogs do, sniffs and squats and ambles, then abruptly tears off to a distant point, leaving me to squint after her, and to follow. Eventually, I make out the forms of two figures on a bench, both unmoving enough to resemble statues. The closer I get, the more the figures take on a familiar shape. Something inside me lifts. I've not seen them for many months. Missy is at their feet as they retrieve from their pockets the treats they carry with them still, either as a reminder or perhaps simply out of habit.

'Hello,' I say.

'Sit,' he tells me, patting the bench.

'Hot day today,' she says, and I agree. 'Yes it was.'

They ask about Missy, and I recount her near-death experience. They look down at her with such fondness that she is instantly forgiven.

Elizabeth nudges me. 'Pavlov's off out on a date later.'

'A date? Really?'

It's still light enough for me to see that Pavlov blushes. He shakes his head firmly.

'Not date,' he corrects.

'He's going for a drink with Agatha,' she tells me. 'On a date.'

'No. I will take coffee, and she will take coffee. Just two friends having coffee, that is all.'

Elizabeth smiles warmly, takes my hand in hers, and squeezes.

For a while, nobody speaks. Each of us just sits here with our eyes closed, heads angled up, drinking in the last of the day's sun, vitamin D levels rising within us like mercury in a thermometer. Missy is at my feet, her flank resting heavily against my shin to let me know that she is there. The street beyond seems unusually quiet, few cars, the occasional arriving bus largely devoid of passengers. The parakeets are coming home for the night to roost, the foxes impatient for darkness to fall. Pavlov says something at which Elizabeth chuckles receptively, and then, in the easy and unthinking way we've developed over these past few years, we fall into habitual conversation, one punctuated by jokes and observations, vivid pronouncements and meandering asides. It's the kind of talk that says both nothing and everything at once, and which feels, here, right now, as precious to me as all the gold in all the banks all across this confounding world.

'Look,' Elizabeth says, pointing.

The light as it dapples through the trees is bewitching.

Acknowledgements

When I first got a dog, I didn't realise just how big a part she would play in establishing for me a new, and not entirely unwelcome, social circle. Through her I met a great many people, and on otherwise humdrum weekday after-noons in the park I enjoyed some unexpectedly stimulating conversations. A few quite strange ones, too. They filled me up, sparked my imagination, and kept me coming back for more. I appreciate all those I encountered, the dogs that came with them, and the friends I made. They are not easily forgotten.

Thank you to Kate Hewson at John Murray, for her keen eye, her instinctive understanding, and for bringing such enthusiasm and wise counsel to the project. Also to her colleagues Lauren Howard, Caroline Westmore, Laurence Cole and Howard Davies for sound and sensitive copy-editing; to Charlotte Hutchinson and Ellie Bailey for press and marketing; to Alice Tait for the lovely illustrations; and to Sally Muir and Sara Marafini for the wonderful cover design. I am endlessly grateful to Lisa Aldwinckle for helping me find my voice. My daughters Amaya and Evie amaze and impress me constantly, and fill me with such pride. Elena: all the words, all the sentiments, all the feelings. And Missy, my beautiful dog, who makes me smile each day, and who's always, *always* keen. Let's go, shall we?